OXFORD
INDIA SHORT
INTRODUCTIONS

RELIGION IN INDIA

The Oxford India Short
Introductions are concise,
stimulating, and accessible guides
to different aspects of India.
Combining authoritative analysis,
new ideas, and diverse perspectives,
they discuss subjects which are
topical yet enduring, as also
emerging areas of study and debate.

SOME OTHER TITLES IN THE SERIES

Employment in India
Ajit Kumar Ghose

Indian Federalism
Louise Tillin

Surrogacy
Anindita Majumdar

Jawaharlal Nehru
Rudrangshu Mukherjee

The Partition of India
Haimanti Roy

Indian Nuclear Policy
Harsh V. Pant and Yogesh Joshi

Indian Democracy
Suhas Palshikar

Indian National Security
Chris Ogden

Bollywood
M. K. Raghavendra

The Indian Middle Class
Surinder S. Jodhka and Aseem Prakash

Indian Foreign Policy
Sumit Ganguly

Dalit Assertion
Sudha Pai

For more information, visit our website:
https://global.oup.com/academic/content/ser
ies/o/oxford-india-short-introductions-ser
ies-oisi/?lang=en&cc=in

OXFORD
INDIA SHORT
INTRODUCTIONS

RELIGION IN INDIA

VARUNI BHATIA

OXFORD
UNIVERSITY PRESS

OXFORD
UNIVERSITY PRESS

Great Clarendon Street, Oxford, OX2 6DP,
United Kingdom

Oxford University Press is a department of the University of Oxford.
It furthers the University's objective of excellence in research, scholarship,
and education by publishing worldwide. Oxford is a registered trade mark of
Oxford University Press in the UK and in certain other countries.

© Varuni Bhatia 2025

The moral rights of the author have been asserted.

Published in the United States of America by Oxford University Press
198 Madison Avenue, New York, NY 10016, United States of America.

British Library Cataloguing in Publication Data
Data available

Library of Congress Control Number: 2025930988

ISBN 978–0–19–895834–5

DOI: 10.1093/oso/9780198958345.001.0001

Pod

The manufacturer's authorized representative in the EU for product safety is Oxford
University Press España S.A., Parque Empresarial San Fernando de Henares,
Avenida de Castilla, 2 – 28830 Madrid (www.oup.es/en).

Contents

Preface

If you have picked up this short introduction and are reading its first lines, you are almost certain to have observed the vastness of the subject and contrasted it with the relatively small size of this book. But then, any book on religion in India, big or small, is faced with this problem of inadequacy. This book, therefore, makes no quixotic pretension at completeness vis-à-vis its subject matter. Rather, it lays out the topos of religion in India—its social and conceptual landscape, as it were—such that it facilitates a broad understanding for an interested explorer of how religion operates in Indian society.

India is home to almost every major religion in the world. According to the last census record, from 2011, the Indian population is made up of 79.8% Hindus, 14.2% Muslims, 2.3% Christians, 1.7% Sikhs, 0.7% Buddhists, 0.4% Jains, 0.7% Other

Religions and Persuasions (ORP), and 0.2% Religion Not Stated.[1] Under ORP fall Jews, Parsis, and those who return themselves as animists. Typically, the list of World Religions—a key concept and category in the discipline of Religious Studies—consists of the following religious traditions: Buddhism, Christianity, Hinduism, Islam, Jainism, Judaism, Sikhism, and Zoroastrianism. More recently in the history of the discipline, this list has started to include Confucianism, Taoism, Shinto, as well as beliefs and practices that fall beyond the frameworks of scripture-based traditions to include categories such as Animism, Paganism, Tribal and Folk religions.

The idea of World Religions has its origin in the academic study of religion in Euro-American universities. Beginning in the mid- to late nineteenth century, Departments of Religion, or Comparative Religions, were established in several major universities in Europe and, later, in the United States. The aim of these departments and other adjacent departments, such as those specializing in oriental languages, anthropology, and, later, area studies, was

---

[1] 'RGI releases Census 2011 data on Population by Religious Communities', https://pib.gov.in/newsite/printrelease.aspx?relid=126 326#:~:text=Total%20Population%20in%202011%20is,Stated%20 0.29%20crores%20(0.2%25). Accessed 24 May 2024.

to engage with the cultural, religious, and language traditions of peoples across the globe. It was a lofty aim, but one that was nonetheless mired in the global power dynamics of Western colonialism and imperialism (Sharpe 1975; Masuzawa 2005). The discipline of Comparative Religion, or Religious Studies (sometimes also called History of Religions), hence, saw its birth in a cauldron of an unequal political and economic world order. However, it also ironically made the first attempts to place the religious traditions it had nominated as World Religions on an equal footing—or, at the very least, tried to locate characteristics or features common to them all. In the process, the discipline itself reified 'religion' as an object of study, turning it into a stand-alone thing by separating it from its embeddedness in a broader field of culture, society, law, and history. Religion, thus, became sui generis, self-created, and a phenomenon in human society that had always been present (McCutcheon 1997).

The other reason why the study of religion found its own institutional space in Euro-American academia is the historical secularization that universities underwent between the sixteenth and the nineteenth centuries in these geographies, clearly separating the remit of the seminary and the university as institutional and intellectual spaces. The university became the site where non-denominational and comparative study of all religions of the world was promoted. Such studies were meant to displace the underlying superiority of a theological, particularly a Protestant Christian, framework of understanding the religious lives and worlds of people across the globe. However, mired in the history of colonialism, the discipline retained Eurocentrism, and an underlying notion of Western superiority, through most of the twentieth century (Masuzawa 2005).

In India, for the most part, Religious Studies does not exist in the university system as an academic discipline. The study of religion is subsumed within the traditional social science and humanities disciplines—most prominently in sociology, anthropology, political science, history, philosophy, and, sometimes, language and literature departments. Historically, modern enquiries into religion thrived outside academia. Several Indian public figures from the late nineteenth and early twentieth centuries drew upon Hindu spirituality as the basis of national identity, while relegating the substantial Muslim population of India to mere numbers and representation. The period was marked by vigorous debates around religion, nation, and society. However, this vibrant public life of religion did not translate into religion being included as an academic discipline in Indian universities, even as faith-based education was widely being provided in schools as well as institutions of higher education, depending upon the religious affiliation of the said institute (Narayanan 2015).

Post-Independence, anthropologists, folklorists, and textualists from Western universities flocked to India to study religion—mainly Hinduism and its textual, practical, and performative aspects. Their scholarship paid attention to the questions of faith, belief, and practice of what was being increasingly claimed as one of the oldest religions of the world. Higher education in Independent India, however, largely eschewed the academic study of religion qua religion. This led to the apparent disjuncture between a heavily religious population and a deeply secular academy—a chasm that would only grow in the subsequent decades. Studying religious texts and traditions, hence, either withdrew into the confines of religious institutions that produced deeply orthodox versions of their respective traditions or was done by scholars who were trained in the disciplinary methods of studying 'the other'.

The ironic dimensions of this approach, one that was meant to produce an educated and secular Indian public freed from the constraints of religious tradition, must be obvious to any observer of contemporary India. Religion today has assumed a definitive role in Indian public life as a marker of identity and belonging, as well as an expression of cultural and political majoritarianism. However, there is little space to understand its role in the everyday lives of people, chart the transformations over a period of historical time, or critique its overtly political and covertly cultural usages, except from a narrowly defined secular position that is looked upon with suspicion by believers of all religious traditions.

Would our situation be different today had institutions of higher education in India approached the academic study of religion with a more open mind during the time of nation-building? It is difficult to answer with certainty. However, it can be stated with relative confidence that such an approach would have allowed religious subjects, critics, and practitioners to engage with religion in a manner that did not reduce it to some other thing—a symptom, a reflection, an expression of something *else*—and, thereby, would have facilitated more meaningful dialogues with each other as well. This short introduction is written under the conviction that it is necessary for our polity and society to engage with religion simultaneously from a multidisciplinary and an interfaith perspective, without losing sight of the central object of study.

The organization of chapters in this book reflects this conviction. It begins with a provisional definition of its object of enquiry: religion as a social institution; a world view, and an ethical framework; a series of explanations regarding the self and the universe (Introduction). But religion is also much more than that, and the subsequent chapters explore these other constitutive facets of religion. Chapter 1 foregrounds the historical dynamism of religions. Focusing on the colonial period, the chapter broadly surveys the reconfigurations and changes in religious practice, authority, and identity. Chapter 2 explores how religion intersects with everyday life. Here we will see that expressions and dogma may vary significantly across religious traditions. However, there are also commonalities between religious actors, practices, and narratives that draw upon shared histories, localities, ecologies, social structures, power relations, zones of conflict, and economic conditions.

Religion remains central to, and works in tandem with, how social relations across categories such as caste and gender unfold in our society, giving rise to some of the more unique expressions of Indian religious life— such as the figure of the guru. Chapter 3 deals with these regularities of religious life and living in India. Law and media are addressed in Chapters 4 and 5, respectively. These two social systems and cultural constructs have played a constitutive role in framing the religious life worlds of the multitudes in India over the last century or so, especially in determining and regulating how religious publics and politics have emerged and operated. The short introduction ends with a reflection on the way forward with regard to religion in our nation.

This book also implicates a certain field of scholarship on religion through the suggestions it makes for further reading on various themes and concerns. In-text citations have been used to point the readers to the sources that have inspired certain strands of thought, arguments, and other information that the book draws from and refers to. A fuller reference to these books and articles can be found in the list of additional readings at the end.

The aim of this short introduction is to step away from studying religion as sui generis, as a 'thing' that has always already been present, as a single and singular phenomenon best located in texts and scriptures. Here, we understand religion through a multidisciplinary and plural perspective, acknowledging the critical role it continues to play in shaping our worlds. It seeks to address a lacuna in the Indian intellectual public sphere around taking religion critically and seriously as an important aspect of the everyday lives of a vast majority of Indians. Finally, it seeks to open a space for understanding and dialogue, without foreclosing the necessary critique of the political use that religion has been put to in recent decades.

Acknowledgements

This short introduction owes its origin to a course on Religion in India that I have now taught for some years. Teaching the course made me realize the need for such a book addressing the Indian context, where the academic study of religion has followed an idiosyncratic trajectory and is distributed across many disciplines. I owe an immense debt to all my students who engaged with religion in all its confounding and bewildering plurality in India with an open-minded curiosity. This book is dedicated to them.

Amit Basole and S. V. Srinivas have been outstanding intellectual companions in the writing of this short introduction. They have served as sounding boards for many of the themes addressed in these pages. S.V. Srinivas, along with Alex Thomas and K. N. Sunandan, read either parts or the whole of this manuscript and gave valuable encouragement and feedback. I have also benefited greatly from my discussions with several colleagues and friends over the years. Bindu Menon, Haimanti Roy, Khalid Anis Ansari, Sharmadip Basu, and Varadarajan Narayanan have been important interlocutors along the way. My wonderful historian colleagues at Azim Premji University—Amit Kumar, Akhila Mathew, D. W. Karuna, Samira Junaid, Sarada Natarajan, Subir Dey, Uthara Suvrathan, and Vinayak—have been a constant source of intellectual vitality. To all of them, I owe more than gratitude; I owe them the world of ideas that has shaped my own.

I am grateful to Arjun Jayadev, former Director, School of Arts and Sciences, Azim Premji University, and Harini Nagendra, former Director, Research Center, Azim Premji University, for providing me with institutional support. Arjun, in particular, has been a constant source of encouragement and support as I tried to complete this book alongside fulfilling my responsibilities at the University.

I would like to express utmost gratitude to my editor, Barun Sarkar, who encouraged me and gave me the confidence to write this short introduction. I thank the three anonymous reviewers of the manuscript for their critical feedback. Barota Hazra, a former student who also took my Religion in India course, helped prepare the manuscript with her characteristic precision and diligence.

As I finish this book, I remain acutely aware of how modest it is, especially when compared to the vastness of the subject under discussion. This must necessarily remain an incomplete discussion. Nonetheless, I hope it is a gratifying one. I take responsibility for all forms of omissions and faults herein.

The content and opinions expressed are those of the author and are not endorsed by, nor do they necessarily reflect the views of, Azim Premji University.

Introduction

Understanding Religion

Writing in the mid-twentieth century, scholar of comparative religion Wilfred Cantwell Smith made this deceptively simple but deeply astute observation:

> Man is everywhere and has always been what we call today 'religious.' Yet there are today and have been in the past relatively few languages into which one can translate the word 'religion'—and particularly its plural 'religions'—outside Western civilization (Smith 1991: 18)

Smith was amongst the first scholars of religion to bring to our attention the fact that the term 'religion' itself was not indigenous to several languages of the world. For many people, he argued, it was not necessary to

Religion in India. Varuni Bhatia, Oxford University Press.
© Varuni Bhatia 2025. DOI: 10.1093/oso/9780198958345.003.0001

know this term, or its semantic equivalences identified in different languages, in order to lead a life that could be recognized as a religious one. In his monumental work, *The Meaning and End of Religion* (1962), Smith argued that the original Latin term, *religare*, changed over centuries to assume the meaning that it has today. A term used by the Romans to refer to rites that bound communities together, during the early Christian centuries it came to refer specifically to monastic vows. Only later did it encompass faith in God. With the Age of Discovery, the Reformation, and the Scientific Revolution, religion, now at home in most European vernaculars, came to denote a true faith in God. Religion was closely associated, if not identified with Protestant Christianity, in the dawn of modernity in Europe. The earlier accusation of 'false religion,' reserved for Jews and Muslims—people of the Book who had strayed away from true faith—continued to persist, now expanded to include all forms of 'irrational' religions, purportedly based on superstition and idolatry.

Gradually, over the nineteenth century, the idea that all humans could have a recognizable form of faith or religion, became widespread amongst European intellectual circles. The process by which 'religion' became a term that denotes a universal human impulse was long and circuitous. It was also one whereby Christian, particularly Protestant Christian, notions of religion emerged as the paradigm within which all other religions of the world would be arranged sequentially and judged. The process involved centuries of asymmetrical contact and exchange, often under the umbrella of colonialism and its attendant forms of inequality and violence (Chidester 2014). Within this expanded definition, 'religion' was delinked from the Christian ecclesiastical and theological framework to include belief in supernatural being/s or states (God/s), a set of practices (rituals), rule book/s governing social, ritual, and moral life (doctrine and scripture), origin stories (myth), death and afterlife (eschatology), and a community of believers. Much of this shift in the meaning and scope of the term 'religion' took place during the long nineteenth century, under the aegis of the spread of colonialism and the simultaneous rise of comparative religion as a discipline in Western academia. God, faith, and scripture became the hallmarks of religion.

Amongst English speakers and speakers of Romance languages across the world, the term 'religion' is well known and circulates seamlessly. However, it is not a term that translates with such ease into other languages of the world. Google Translate shows 'religion' as *dharma/dharam* in Sanskrit and Sanskrit-derived languages, *madham* in Tamil, *mazhab* in Urdu, and *din* in Arabic and Persian. All these terms enjoy purchase in the linguistically diverse Indian context. Amongst non-English terms, the Sanskrit-Pali derived *dharma/ dharam/dhamma* is the most widely used, and understood, as 'religion' in contemporary India. This is borne out by several broad surveys (e.g., the Census, the Pew Survey) where both 'religion' and *dharma* were used in questionnaires depending upon whether the survey was being conducted in English or other Indian languages. While being widely and popularly understood as referring to the same phenomenon as the term 'religion', none of these, it is important to note, strictly refer to what 'religion' means in English—i.e., a Protestant complex of God, faith, sacred text, and a community of believers. In this regard, the Latin-derived term is novel and unique in the Indian context—a result of India's colonial encounter. It is also a term that draws its immense power from the translation of the Western concept into the radically different and diffused religious landscape of pre-colonial India.

The translation of 'religion' into *dharma* in Indian languages was carried out in a systematic fashion by nineteenth-century elites, in whose writings terms such as *Hindu dharma* or *Sanatan dharma* became popular as a means of referring to the phenomenon we today call Hinduism. However, 'religion'—understood as a conglomeration of a creator God, faith, scripture, and community held together by all of the above—was not entirely applicable in the Indian context. The interchangeability of the terms 'religion' and *dharma* was, according to some, an act of mistranslation and epistemological violence imposed by a colonial state and Christian missionaries (Balagangadhara 1994). In this context, it is important to state that the idea that religion is a universal human phenomenon, or even that there is a universal religion—a common set of characteristics or features that together constitutes something called 'religion'—is relatively new, not more than two hundred years old. It is meaningful to turn to an example from a different continent altogether to comprehend this transformation in the history of ideas fully. For the first European explorers of America in the sixteenth century, the indigenous people of that continent did not have any religion at all—the only religion at the time for the Europeans was Christianity, while all other faiths were either 'false' religions or forms of paganism and heathenism that the Romans and Greeks of ancient civilizations followed. Similarly, for European travellers to India in the early modern period, the religion of its common people was either a wrongful form of true Christian faith or a form of idolatry that was practised by the Romans during ancient times.

In the nineteenth and early twentieth century, with the development of natural and humanistic sciences and the emergence of academic disciplines such as Sociology, Philology, and Psychology, analytical frameworks to understand religion emerged. While these analytical frameworks did not replace older theological, even experiential, approaches towards religion, they did allow scholars to understand religion and the role it plays in society in a secular, i.e. non-confessional, fashion. All religions, French sociologist Émile Durkheim pointed out in his landmark study *The Elementary Forms of Religious Life* (first published in French in 1912), have to do with the idea of the *sacred*—which he defined as 'things set apart and forbidden' (Durkeim 1995: 44). Around such objects and ideas 'set apart' or 'forbidden', Durkheim argued, grows a community that collectively recognizes them as sacred—this community is what he calles a 'Church'. Since a broad social community around sacredness lay at the heart of religion—a community that needed to be (re)produced time and again, Durkheim concluded that religion ought to be understood as an 'eminently social thing' (Durkheim 1995: 9).

Writing about religion decades before Durkheim, Karl Marx also understood religion through the lens of a sociological framework, and as a product of the human social fabric. For Marx, though, religion was a system that obscured objective socio-economic relations of exploitation (Pals 2006). Simultaneously, religion produced in the exploited classes a dependence on it by providing temporary relief and succour in the manner of a consciousness-altering drug. Sigmund Freud turned to the inner workings of the human mind to explain religion primarily as 'an illusion', a set of rules and regulations that keep humans within the ambit of civilization. Once the rational human mind has emerged in its fullest capacity, Freud suggested, like Marx, that religion would lose its significance and fade away (Freud 1927).

Not all scholars were satisfied with theories of religion that explained it away as a remnant of an unscientific and irrational past. Beginning with European orientalists in the later eighteenth century, scholars of comparative religions during the late nineteenth and early twentieth century tried to find common ground between different religions of the world. This increasingly led to an understanding that there exists a common pool of ideas around expressions of faith towards a superior being. Friedrich Max Muller, amongst the most influential scholars of comparative religion from this period, insisted that there was a universal strain of belief that ran through all of humanity—scholars simply needed to find its particular expression in each society. And thus, in the late nineteenth century, a set of World Religions, purportedly covering the entire world's population, were identified. By the early twentieth century, the older notion of belief was replaced by the unpredictable, albeit irreducible, sense of awe in the face of a mystical enormity as the basis of a common religious experience. William James, the American philosopher and psychologist, asserted in his *Varieties of Religious Experience* (1902), that mysticism or religious experience lay at the heart of all religions. In *The Idea of the Holy* (first published in German in 1917), the German scholar of comparative religions Rudolf Otto argued that all religions were united by *mysterium tremendum*—a sense of awe and mystery in the face of what humans considered to be beyond comprehension, which he called the 'numinous'.

India and Comparative Religion

One of the abiding influences on the public narrative of religion in India—and one that had far-reaching consequences in the context of comparative religions—was the fifty-volume *Sacred Books of the East* (1879–1910) by German Indologist and philologist Friedrich Max Muller. He propagated the idea that Eastern religions were no less worthy of scholarly attention than Abrahamic traditions; they had their own epistemological and theological claims worth considering, their own scriptures, and a community of believers who were, at their core, far from mere idolatrous pagans. Max Muller and his fellow nineteenth-century orientalists, philologists, and linguists had brought India and Indian religions into the realm of comparative religions. Their translations, scholarly writings, ethnographic accounts, and philological and linguistic endeavours successfully put India and its religious traditions, especially those deriving from classical texts written in Sanskrit and Pali, firmly within the ambit of the newly emerging academic study of religion in the Euro-American academy.

An unexpected outcome of this was that religion emerged as one of the prime scholarly sites of engaging with India in the twentieth century. From the perspective of this discipline, the story of modern India could be narrated through the interactions and dialogues between the world's three major religions: Hinduism, Christianity, and Islam. Within Religious Studies, colonial and especially postcolonial India was understood primarily as the home of one of the most important world religions—Hinduism. This understanding of India as a religious—and primarily a Hindu—country, was built upon older orientalist notions of Hindu mysticism and spirituality (King

2013). In nineteenth-century European writings on India, religion was also seen as India's predominant explanatory framework, alongside climate. Within this framework, Hinduism represented the oldest and indigenous faith of the land, Islam represented the powers of conquerors and oppressors, and Christianity stood for rational faith, progress, and the beneficent winds of modern change (Metcalf 1997). By the twentieth century, both for Hindu reformers and for the colonizers, India became fixed as the land of spirituality and mysticism, of ancient sages and their lofty teachings.

For several Indians in the early decades of the twentieth century, religion was very much a part of public life. It was not divorced from questions of ethics, culture, belonging, and the nation. One of the most prominent spokespersons for Hinduism at this time was Swami Vivekananda whose lectures and public speeches cemented his place globally as a charismatic Hindu monk and leader. His teachings, based on the philosophical system of Vedanta, invoked a sense of religious universalism and appealed greatly to the Western public hungry to learn about Eastern traditions. No other public religious figure from this period has done more than Swami Vivekananda in establishing Vedantic non-dualism as the core teaching of Hinduism. At the same time, there were also

Indians who thought broadly about religion, outside its cultural and national moorings. Echoing William James in a series of lectures delivered at Oxford in 1930, India's national poet Rabindranath Tagore identified religion as the experience of the divine, who he called *moner manush*, or 'the Man of the Heart' (Tagore 1931). Tagore dipped into the vast ocean of Bengal's popular religious traditions to find strains of a universal experience of the divine. In his copious writings, S. Radhakrishnan found in religion, particularly in classical Hindu traditions, the grounds for forging universal brotherhood, world peace, and rational faith (Radhakrishnan 1927). Muhammad Iqbal understood Islam as a universal ethical force beyond the realms of nations and nationalism (Sevea 2012). In his writings as well as his life, Gandhi steadfastly held on to religion as a key source of spirituality and morality that informed his politics (Rao 1978). He remained a practising and believing Hindu throughout his life.

However, the public discourse on religion in India in the early decades of the twentieth century was not all laudatory of the purported spiritualism of Hinduism and Eastern religious traditions. There were critics, too. Building upon existing critiques of Hinduism by the likes of Jotiba Phule and Iyothee Thass from the previous century, E. V. Ramaswamy

Naicker, better known as Periyar, promoted a rationalist's approach towards religion. Periyar, for his part, based his critique not only on an atheistic standpoint but also on what he identified as an essential feature of Hindu tradition—its caste-based oppression (Geetha and Rajadurai 1998). Periyar's political legacy was taken up by the Dravidian movement. The intellectual and reformist aspects of Periyar's ideas were diffused across India in a series of rationalists' societies that continue to bring together caste critique of Hindu traditions alongside a scientific rationality expressed as atheism.

One of the sharpest minds of twentieth-century India on the topic of religion was Dr B. R. Ambedkar. He was also one of the few thinkers and public intellectuals who understood the key role played by religion in forging communities, especially in providing these communities with a social bond and a moral framework. Ambedkar pointedly criticized Hinduism as a religion that validated an unequal social order. However, he was unwilling to give up on the larger moral universe and social fabric that he believed religion should be able to provide to its adherents (Jondhale and Beltz 2004). Hence, in the last few years of his life, Ambedkar accepted initiation into Buddhism which, he held, had historically posed a challenge to the unequal social universe found in Brahmanical texts and classical Hindu traditions.

Conclusion

It is clear from the above discussion that religion emerged in twentieth-century India as a public and fraught category—a far cry from its private and faith-based articulations in the modern West. In India, it indicated a host of social, cultural, moral, and political dimensions that were, and continue to be, in excess of the individual and rational faith of Enlightenment religion that had purportedly been ushered into modern Europe. This privatization of religion into the realm of individual faith, and its attendant separation from state and polity in several Western European countries over the nineteenth and twentieth centuries, allowed the modern West, to lay the grounds of what a paradigmatic secular polity and society would look like, at least in theory if not in practice. For reasons indicated above, and those that will be discussed in the forthcoming pages, this particular kind of secularism did not take root in India. Over the next few chapters, we shall understand these public aspects of religion in India in the manner in which they were articulated, contested, and established in contemporary India. Rather than approach religion through a purely scripturalist or doctrinaire perspective, thereby turning it into an object of study, the remaining chapters will explore religion thematically and through an intertwined set of relationships between history, praxis, law, media, and civil society.

1

Religion, Modernity, Identity

While faith, belief, ritual practices, sacred spaces, myth, and philosophy are neither modern nor unique to any particular tradition, the term 'religion' certainly is. One of the more abiding factors of religion in the modern world, and especially in modern India, has been its immense ability to be deployed as a marker identity. With a few exceptions, every ten years since 1871, Indians have been asked to identify which religion they belong to. The most recent census data collected in 2011 shows that a numerical majority of Indians identify themselves as Hindu. The second largest religious group in India are the Muslims, with the adherents of all other religions—Christians, Sikhs, Buddhists, Jains, and Others—forming a relatively smaller proportion of India's total population. Together, however,

Religion in India. Varuni Bhatia, Oxford University Press.
© Varuni Bhatia 2025. DOI: 10.1093/oso/9780198958345.003.0002

non-Hindus consist of a substantial minority in the country, standing currently at about 20%. This minority is not evenly distributed across the country. For example, according to the report on the distribution of populations according to religions, an overwhelming majority of India's approximately 2% Sikh population resides in the state of Punjab, while Assam, Uttar Pradesh, West Bengal, and Kerala have a substantial Muslim population, higher than the national average. Kashmir and Lakshadweep, both Union Territories at the time of publication of this book, are the only parts of India where Muslims are in a majority. Similarly, the north-eastern states of Nagaland, Mizoram, Manipur, Sikkim, and Arunachal Pradesh, alongside states like Tamil Nadu, host a substantial Christian population (ORGI 2011). The uneven distribution of adherents of different religions across various states, regions, and linguistic communities in India is a significant aspect of the diversity of Indian society—perhaps no less important than the inherent religious plurality of the society itself. Another unevenness that we can identify is the disparate spheres of influence borne by different religious groups in India, in contemporary times as well as in the past. Hence, while Jainism today may consist of barely 4–5 million adherents in India according to the 2011 Census, their influence in Indian society and economy far exceeds their numerical presence.

Today, we can easily turn to the census to find demographic data pertaining to religion in India. We can access the exact numbers of people belonging to any religious community residing in any state, district, municipality, or panchayat in the country. We may even be able to access this information at a neighbourhood level with the right combination of publicly available resources. Census data assumes unanimity and homogeneity around the question of religious identity. Those of us who access this data, whether as curious citizens or as policymakers, similarly accept the validity of the categories used in the data unquestioningly. However, even up to a hundred years ago, the answer to the question of religious identity was not uniformly clear. For instance, in the context of collecting the Census of 1911, the census commissioner of India, Colonel Gait, admitted that the category 'Hindu' was an unclear one (Datta 1999). The problem was not merely with defining who was a Hindu. It impacted Sikhs as well, whose numbers swung enormously in various census data from the late nineteenth to the early twentieth century. And several communities who were neither clearly nor visibly Muslim or Christian were often automatically categorized as Hindu. However, and despite these discrepancies that would take decades to settle, it was clear by the first decades of the twentieth century that religion as identity would remain a lasting feature of Indian social and political life. This was, in and of itself, a key transformation of the role that both religion and identities had in pre-colonial India.

Pre-Colonial Identities and Religion

In the colonial period, religion emerged in India as the primary marker of identity. Prior to that, it was one of several kinds of collective networks of belonging that included caste, language, ethnicity, and region. The 'constant interplay and overlap between Islamicate and Indic worldviews' shaped how ordinary people in pre-colonial India dealt with intercommunity inter-actions (Gilmartin and Lawrence 2000: 2). Extant evidence from the twelfth to the eighteenth centuries points to the usage of ethnic and caste-based identifi-catory terms such as 'Turk', 'Pathan', 'Maratha', and 'Rajput' as a way to refer to a kin group. In fact, the term 'Hindu', itself of Persian provenance, was pri-marily an ethnic marker used by foreign travellers to speak of the people who lived across the river Indus, i.e., Sindhu. Certain broad-based caste groups could be found across religious boundaries—such as the Jats in north India. Around the end of the seventeenth century, a large number of Jats—a pastoral community that had settled into agriculture in the fertile Punjab region—became *sikh* (or disciples) of Guru Gobind Singh, the tenth guru in the lineage of Guru Nanak (Oberoi 1994). Similarly, in eastern India, over the seventeenth and eighteenth centuries, a large number of forest-dwelling people who resided in the marshy Gangetic delta region embraced Islam under the influence of Sufi *pirs* who came with the knowledge of indigenous medicine and forest-clearing, and assisted in the eastwards spread of the rice-cultivation frontier of the subcontinent (Eaton 1993).

A pertinent question to ask here is: were the agriculturalists who became Sikh, and the indigenous peoples of eastern India who became Muslim, all 'Hindus' who converted to a different religion? That would be the narrow view of the processes that led to such religious affiliations. It is far more enabling to think of people's religious adherence through the prism of the fluidity and praxis that allows us to attend to local contexts. When we do so, it is not clear if we can speak of premodern identities as exclusive and singular in the same way that we do for modern identities. Manu Devadevan shows in his recent work how 'religious identities were created as a result of formidable historical processes' over the early medieval period, in what he calls the prehistory of Hinduism (Devadevan 2016: 11). This includes dialogues between classical philosophical traditions, monastic institutions, imperial centres such as the Vijayanagara empire and new innovations in political economy that led to the emergence of new class formations. If we turn to the vast corpus of medieval devotional poetry—the first corpus of literature composed by the 'common people' of India to come down to us—we find a similar trend. Kabir considered himself a weaver, a *julaha*, just as Namdev called himself a *simpi*, a tailor, while Basavanna identified himself as a *jangama*, a person who is constantly on the move. How else should we understand that Mirabai was a royal princess from western India, Chaitanya a Brahmin from Nabadwip, and Ravidas a leather-worker from Banaras? All three would fall under the category of 'Hindu' in today's census records. If we step back even further into Indian history, we find evidence of a surprising disregard for exclusive religious identities carried over generations, especially amongst the ruling elite. Ashoka was a well-known Buddhist, but his father Chandragupta Maurya was supposedly a Jain who, legend says, performed the austere practice of *sallekhana* (ceasing to eat and drink) at the Jain sacred site at Sravanabelagola in Karnataka. The caves of the early Rashtrakuta and Chalukya rulers at Badami show the interpermeation of Jain, Buddhist, and Hindu religious affiliations in these ruling families. Dara Shikoh was a Mughal prince and an elite Muslim who translated the *Upanishads* into Persian, while his great-grandfather Akbar went as far as to initiate his own mystical order, proclaiming himself to be the prophet who was supposed to arrive a millennia after Prophet Muhammad.

The above examples are not meant to paint a romantic picture of a tolerant, peaceful, and conflict-free past. Rather, they are meant to demonstrate that religion was one amongst a complex set of markers which individuals and communities used to identify themselves. Premodern identities were not reducible exclusively to religion, just as religion included elements of praxis as much as of textually driven faith. Besides, religion itself was plural and fluid in practice, especially by non-elite and subaltern groups in the Indian subcontinent prior to the establishment of an enumerative colonial state, driven by collecting data about its subjects. The emergence of modern religious sensibilities in India, under the aegis of colonialism, is strongly intertwined with the formation of what Sudipta Kaviraj has called imagined, exclusive, and idealist religious communities, 'bodies of Hindus and Muslims, which formed the primary and indissoluble units of social beings and action, with the close implication that, by definition, these communities could not live harmoniously together' (Kaviraj 1997: 328). The process of the emergence of religion as a marker of identity and primary community was forged by the enumerative practices of the colonial state and encouraged by nineteenth-century religious reform and revivalist movements.

Colonial Modernity and Religious Reform Movements

The nineteenth century is key to understanding the way religion emerges as the primary identity and basis of community for people of the Indian subcontinent. During the nineteenth century, and as a result of colonial rule, a series of legal processes, government policies, political ideologies, and moral frameworks were introduced into the subcontinent that led to significant transformations in the religious worlds inhabited by Indians thus far. Religion, especially the primacy of religion as identity, the uniformity accorded to various religious traditions across vast regional and linguistic registers, as well as the breakdown of a fluid and layered sense of self and community were an integral part of nineteenth-century transformations.

The colonial transformation of religion in the Indian subcontinent can be identified under the interrelated frameworks of religious reform and revival, law and governance, and cultural nationalism. By and large, the colonial state in India operated as a governing mechanism vis-à-vis India's religious groups and traditions. It wanted to regulate religious practices within a utilitarian framework of good governance which would also cause least upheaval in law and order. Its early reformist approach towards abolishing religiously sanctioned cultural practices such as *sati* or *sahamarana* amongst high-caste Hindus (where the widow would burn alongside the body of her husband, outlawed in 1829), gradually gave way to a more hands-off approach towards religion in subsequent decades. Even then, legal reforms that brought about progressive measures such as widow remarriage and increasing the age of consent for marriage for Hindu girls ensured that the colonial state continued to regulate the religiously sanctioned social life of its subjects—an issue that caused a high degree of discontent amongst early anti-colonial nationalists. In the process, the state also understood and interpreted religion specifically within a scriptural framework. It reduced the myriad local, regional, and caste-based practices to mere deviations from what was enjoined in sacred law books.

The East India Company's endeavour to find the 'original' and 'most accurate' version of Hindu and Muslim social practices in their scriptures led to a massive translation and commentarial industry in the late eighteenth and early nineteenth centuries (Breckenridge and van der Veer 1993; Dalmia 2003). Spurred on by the efforts of a group of scholar-administrators known as the orientalists, a vast array of Sanskrit and a selection of Persian texts were translated into English and other European languages. Amongst these were the *Bhagavad Gita*, Manu's *Dharmashastra*, the *Vishnu Purana*, the plays of Kalidasa, the *Tarikh-i-Farishta* (The History by Farishta), and commentaries as well as law books. Orientalist scholar-administrators were actively assisted by *pandits*, *dubashis* (those familiar with two languages), *maulavis*, and experts in Persian language in their endeavours. This meant that their understanding of the two religious traditions of Hinduism and Islam was deeply influenced by a classical and scriptural perspective. While both Sanskrit and Persian manuscripts were collected and sometimes studied by East India Company officers and scholar-administrators, the tendency to view Sanskrit as the repository of authentic Indian religion and culture remained high, while Persian texts were seen to be important primarily as translations of Sanskrit texts, or as histories. In turn, these translations were studied by future generations of administrators being trained in elite schools in England to rule India, reproducing a body of administrators who understood India as predominantly Hindu in a classical and scriptural sense (Inden 1990).

Not only were Hindu and Muslim practices different across regional, caste, and linguistic communities, there was hardly any single institutional authority across the Indian subcontinent that served as a centralizing authority with regard to doctrinal matters. The centrifugal nature of Hinduism, in particular, was deeply confounding for the colonial state, and would lead to unevenness in administrative policies, legal measures, and governing mechanisms in the nineteenth century. It was out of this cauldron of unequal exchange that some of the earliest Hindu reform movements, such as the Tattvabodhini Sabha and the Brahmo Samaj, were born in early nineteenth-century Bengal (Hatcher 2014). Responding to European—chiefly evangelical but also utilitarian—critiques of religion from the vantage point of rational faith, the early reformist movements—which were composed of an elite and wealthy group of upper-caste Bengalis, many of whom had made their fortunes under new colonial policies around land and trade—attempted to redefine Hinduism within the framework of

Enlightenment, thereby privileging monotheism and rational faith (Halbfass 1988). A critique of idolatry, rituals, priestly authority, and the everyday practices of Hinduism—alongside considering scripture as the sole and last authority—was a part of this complex and rapidly transforming landscape (Yelle 2013). After the Mutiny of 1857, Muslim reform movements also started to constrain customary practices, such as visiting dargahs or venerating *pirs*, that were seen to be against the tenets of scriptural Islam (Metcalf 1982).

In this ecology of asymmetrical power between colonial rulers and subjects, one must introduce another key actor—Christian missionaries. Post-Reformation Christianity assumed a serious commitment towards evangelical activity across the globe. In the seventeenth and eighteenth centuries, Christian missionaries travelled, alongside merchants and traders and colonialists, to remote and often difficult parts of the world in order to spread the Gospel. Evangelizing activities began in India in earnest in the mid-to-late eighteenth century—although Christians of various denominations had been present in the subcontinent since much earlier (Frykenberg 1993). While evangelical success was limited when it came to the number of conversions to Christianity, the missionaries were able to shift the discourse around religion in a significant fashion in the Indian subcontinent. The late nineteenth-century Hindu revivalist and reformist movements—the Arya Samaj in western India, the modern reformulation of Gaudiya Vaishnavism in Bengal, the Sanatan Dharma Rakshini Sabha of north India, SNDP (Sree Narayana Dharma Paripalana) Yogam movement in Kerala, Swaminarayan sect in Gujarat, the Ramakrishna Mission in Bengal, and other such socio-religious organizations across India—were contextualized, amongst other things, within dialogue, often unequal and of a highly polemical kind on both sides, between Hindu spokespersons and Christian missionaries (Sharma 2005). By the end of the nineteenth century, Hinduism had emerged as a homogenous, monotheistic, and rational faith founded in the eternal teachings of Vedanta, whose metaphysical aspects evolved in the *Upanishads*, and whose key scripture was the *Bhagavad Gita* (Davis 2015; Mukul 2015). This is not to deny the deep and long historical roots of various religious traditions we broadly identify as Hindu, but merely to indicate that the manner in which they come together as aspects of the one religion called Hinduism is a product of colonial modernity and its intellectual and administrative mechanisms (Hatcher 2016).

One of the more widespread misconceptions that we have when thinking of nineteenth-century religious reform movements in India is that they were concerted, largely homogenous movements with a single-pointed agenda. However, the story is much more complicated than that. Not only did the terms 'reform' and 'revival' mean different things to different actors, but there were also regional differences located in local contexts. For instance, the Arya Samaj fiercely opposed idolatry while the Sanatan Dharma Rakshini Sabha, operating out of the neighbouring Hindi-speaking region, was committed to preserving the rites and practices of orthodox Hinduism—including image-worship (Dalmia 1997). Both these organizations were vehemently opposed to each other in the late nineteenth century but buried their differences in the second decade of the twentieth century in order to present a unified front against the spectre of the Muslim demographic in India. To take another example, Swami Vivekananda and Sree Narayana Guru both turned to Vedanta as the ideal expression of Hindu theology, while remaining strongly rooted in their local contexts to inform their reformist, educational, and service programme. What is significant is that every single socio-religious movement of this period staked its claim to authority over the most authentic form of Hinduism by appealing to classical Hindu scriptures.

The question of social inequality and discrimination often ruptured the straightforward narrative of Hindu religious reform and its attendant claims of Hindu unity. Caste continued to produce a cleavage in the emergent narrative of a homogenous Hinduism in early twentieth-century India (Lee 2021). In southern India, Sree Narayana Guru introduced an underlying caste critique alongside religious reform of the Vedantic kind that drew inspiration from Swami Vivekananda's writings and ideas (Chandramohan 2016). The Ad Dharm movement in United Provinces and the Punjab was popular amongst marginal castes in these regions that continued to resist the overarching narrative of a homogenous and scripturally sanctioned religion, whether Hinduism or Sikhism (Juergensmeyer 1982; Ram 2008). Madras Presidency saw the convergence of traditional non-Brahmin movements with contemporary narratives that identified scriptural Hinduism as the religion of the foreign and conquering 'Aryans' or Brahmins (Pandiyan 2007).

Muslim intellectuals and institutions of modernity, reform, and revival were also responding to and operating within local as well as global imperatives (Metcalf 1982; Robinson 2008). The figure of the Muslim in India remained an aberration of sorts for the colonial state and administrators. While the

British acknowledged that most Muslims in India were converts to Islam, they viewed Islam itself as a creed fundamentally foreign to Indian civilization, one that had arrived, ruled, and grew by the sword, destroying India's Hindu essence and heritage. Grandiosely, the British saw themselves as liberators of the Hindu in India and, as such, provided colonial rule with moral justification. This framework of the indigenous Hindus and foreign, conquering Muslims in India would have far-reaching ramifications that can be seen to this day and was avidly echoed by a range of Indian nationalists. A concocted and inaccurate image, located more in Europe's own history with Islam than within Indian social or political realities, it was already apparent as a stereotype during the period of East India Company's rule in India. Colonial modernity for elite Indian Muslims meant the loss of older sources of prestige and authority and the emergence of a new form of political power that was deeply suspicious of Muslims whom they viewed as a homogenous and rebellious community. After the Mutiny of 1857, it turned into a sophisticated and widely disseminated narrative of Muslim disloyalty. Post-1857, hence, elite Muslim responses to colonialism were strongly embedded within these anxieties. This led to a distinct form of Muslim modernity that was honed within the corridors of institutions like the Muhammadan Anglo-Oriental College at Aligarh, founded by Sir Syed Ahmad Khan—a north Indian aristocrat. Sir Syed advocated that Indian Muslims embrace Western modernity, alongside maintaining the practices of high Muslim culture. The Aligarh school emerged as an immensely influential movement, setting the foundations for elite Muslim modernity and intellectual life in north India that would leave an imprint on twentieth-century politics in the subcontinent (Lelyveld 1975).

Elite Muslims across the world during the colonial period were active and enthusiastic participants in what Nile Green has characterized as 'global Islam'—a unique imagination of a modern, rational faith on a global scale that extended from Beirut and Istanbul to Paris, Bombay, and New York (Green 2020). Assisted by technologies of modern communications—the print media, the telegraph, new and faster modes of travel—global Islam emerged on the shoulders of new religious authorities while simultaneously coming into conflict with the two existing pillars of Islamic authority in various parts of the world—the legal expert or the *ulema* and the charismatic Sufi. It was deeply suspicious of existing local forms of Islam, which often found expression in local shrines and religious practices around such spaces that were denounced as superstitions by the votaries of reformist Islam. The Darul Uloom Deoband was influential as a movement of Islamic traditionalism in the colonial period and had widespread influence across the world. The Deobandi ulema laid particular emphasis on the correct scriptural basis of religious and social practices and attempted to regulate the religious and social life of Muslims by issuing *fatwas*—legal ordinances that bore the stamp of theological authority. A large number of fatwas issued by the Deobandi ulema dealt with the question of quotidian religious practices, especially around Sufi practices such as *zikr* (repetition), venerating the Suri *pir* (spiritual master), pilgrimages to *dargahs* (the graves of Sufi notables), or the celebration of *urs* (death anniversary of the saint). A number of these injunctions were against popular practices of Islam in the subcontinent. They attempted to standardize customary practices that were different across regions and status, and privileged an elite and scriptural form of Islam. By the early twentieth century, the Deobandi seminary had formed a substantial network of seminaries across north India. It played an important role in regulating the religious lives of Muslims across the subcontinent. Alongside the Ahmadiyyas, the Aligarh School (as the Muhammadan Anglo-Oriental College was

being known), the Ahl-i-Hadith, and other movements, the Deobandi seminaries were significant
as institutions of Muslim modernity in the Indian
subcontinent in the early twentieth century.

One of the more fascinating stories of
nineteenth-century formation of modern religious
identities is that of Sikhism. Sikhs, literally 'disciples',
were the followers of Guru Nanak and the ten Sikh
gurus. In the nineteenth century, the Sikhs belonged
to a range of different subgroups, each with their own
doctrinal interpretations of scripture and social-ritual
practices. The most influential amongst the Sikhs were
those who had been through an initiation ceremony
and were considered a part of *Khalsa* (literally, pure).
They considered themselves to be the purest and
most authentic followers of the religion. In the nineteenth century, colonial administrators and scholars
did not uniformly recognize the Sikhs as a distinct
religious identity. Due to the significance of the Sikh
Empire, the Anglo-Sikh Wars of the early nineteenth
century, and later the considerable presence of Sikh
soldiers in the British Indian army, colonial officials
were not unaware of this group. However, they were
often categorized as Hindus in official records such
as the census—especially those Sikhs who did not
visibly demonstrate key identificatory markers such as
unshorn hair and the turban.

In the late nineteenth century, responding to the hegemonic consolidation of Hindu religious identity, particularly under the aegis of the Arya Samaj, there was a concerted effort made by Sikh organizations and individuals to identify themselves as Sikh in colonial records. The Singh Sabhas were founded by Sikhs belonging to established spiritual and political lineages. These Sabhas interpreted scriptures, established scripturally sanctioned practices at Sikh sacred sites, and condemned practices among Sikhs such as goddess worship that were seen to be derived from popular Hinduism. Sikh religious authorities associated with the Singh Sabha movement addressed queries around the practices of everyday Sikhism such as whether or not songs outside the Guru Granth Sahib could be sung in kirtans or whether a low-caste Sikh might be considered equal to a high-caste Sikh. As a result, by the turn of the twentieth century, a modern and scriptural Sikhism was in place (Oberoi 1994).

Numbers, Representation, Communalism: Towards Two Nations

A pivotal feature of religious modernity in the colonial period—onethatwouldhavefar-reachingconsequences on the future of the Indian subcontinent—was the emergence of the 'majority' and 'minority' question vis-à-vis different religious groups in the subcontinent. This was a direct result of colonial policies and approaches to the question of religion in India. In his landmark essay on the colonial census in British India, Bernard Cohn argues that collecting data on its subject population was not an innocent or neutral exercise, but that it made certain classificatory categories used in these censuses appear timeless, hegemonic, and natural, thereby creating conditions for new kinds of identities to be crystallized and new kinds of politics to emerge from these identities (Cohn 1987). Unprecedented primacy was afforded to religious communities by the colonial state and its enumerative logic. Moreover, these religion-based communities were understood as homogenous and singular. And they were recognized as the unit of legal and representative mechanisms. One of the most significant causes of the emergence of the majority–minority narrative was the numbers game inaugurated by the colonial administrative process of collecting census data. In each census, the religious affiliation data of its population was carefully collected and curated by the colonial state.

This exercise led to vast anxiety around numbers amongst both Hindus and Muslims at a time when populations were being demographically mapped and turned into the basis for political representation. In a nation anticipating self-government, Hindu representatives were worried about being reduced to a 'minority' in India—a place they considered to be the 'home' of Hindu religion—while Muslim public figures were concerned about being steam-rolled into a social, cultural, and political ecology of Hindu majoritarianism, with greatly reduced glory and prestige when compared to earlier times. The former expressed exaggerated fears of the so-called Muslim growth rate, blaming it on Muslim social and religious practices. These unfounded anxieties found expression in deeply polarizing, yet popular, books such as U. N. Mukherjee's *A Dying Race* (1929) that cultivated a misplaced sense of diminishing numbers of Hindus and a steadily rising population of Muslims in India. The latter demanded, and received, greater representation than their number allowed for in the legislative assemblies that were increasingly allowing the participation of Indian elected members. In the unfortunately titled Communal Award, which was a part of the Morley–Minto Reforms of 1919, Muslims were given the right to vote in separate constituencies which only Muslim candidates would be allowed to contest. The 1932 Poona Pact between Gandhi and a recalcitrant Ambedkar ensured that the so-called depressed classes accepted being considered 'Hindus' for the sake of political representation. The Poona Pact brought Dalits into the larger Hindu fold for the purpose of political representation—an outcome that has been debated ever since. As a result, Hindu unity in terms of numbers remained undiminished for the purpose of political representation. Population statistics, and the numbers under each religious category, had significant ramifications for how the history of modern India would play out over the next few decades.

By the twentieth century, if there was one term that defined Hindu–Muslim relations in British India, it was 'communalism' (Pandey 1990). This term was used extensively in colonial records from the late nineteenth century to characterize any form of group-driven public disturbance or violence, irrespective of its social or religious nuances. This ideology of communalism, or the primacy given to one's (religious) community, was understood by colonial administrators to determine all forms of social relations in India. The British insistence in locating all fault lines along religious divides in Indian society contrasted with their own loftier ideal of nationalism whereby the nation, and not the religious community, received greater importance. Indians, the British insisted, could never truly be nationalists because they were too loyal to their own religious communities. Furthermore, there was no nation of India that one could even speak of, as Sir John Strachey had noted in oft-quoted passages from his book *India: Its Administration and Progress* (1882). India, according to Strachey, was only a haphazard conglomeration of castes, sects, religions, ethnicities, and languages that could burst out in communal passions, but could hardly muster the higher ideals of nationalism.

In popular writings, this is understood as the 'divide and rule' strategy of the British. The narrative of religious polarization, narrow communal loyalties, and even outright religious and sectarian violence was key to this strategy. Over the next thirty years, the struggle over representation—first in provincial assemblies and later in the Constituent Assembly, the body that would go on to draft independent India's Constitution—raged in a relentless fashion. As religious communities turned into political actors, the idea of a 'nation of one's own' gained strength, culminating in the 'two-nation theory'. This theory, most clearly articulated in Muhammad Iqbal's writings and Muhammad Ali Jinnah's speeches, argued that not only were Hindus and Muslims two different religions and communities, they were also two different nations each deserving their own homeland. The demand for a separate homeland for Indian Muslims would gain strength over the next two decades, based upon the irrefutable logic that within a democracy Muslims would always be fewer in numbers and hence their political significance would also be deeply diminished.

Meanwhile, there were other arguments being made that implicitly supported the two-nation proposal, albeit desiring different outcomes. Vinayak Damodar Savarkar, in his 1923 pseudonymous publication *Who Is a Hindu?* (later published and better known as *Essentials of Hindutva*), strongly argued for the integral territorial unity of the subcontinent based upon its essential Hindu*ness*, or Hindutva. Hindutva referred to the blood relations between various members of its population. Savarkar also pointed out the lack of loyalty of Muslims and Christians, even those who were converts and hence not strictly outsiders, towards this Hindu homeland and holy land (Savarkar 1923). His strong opinion was that Hindus and Muslims were distinct social, cultural, and ethnic groups that were fundamentally irreconcilable. If the Muslim League under Jinnah's two-nation argument called for the partition of British India into two separate nations, those influenced by Hindutva's ideas called for maintaining the territorial integrity of the subcontinent, but with a highly concentrated Hindu cultural inflection to the emergent nation. Civil Society organizations like the Rashtriya Swayamsevak

Sangh (RSS; National Volunteer Corps) were birthed in this historical context with the clear aim of establishing a nation that drew upon ancient Hindu principles of polity and society (Anderson and Damle 1987; Jaffrelot 1996).

The partition of British India was carried out in 1947 on the explicit principle of religious majority. Muslim majority regions from British Indian provinces of the Punjab, Bengal, and Assam were culled out and made into a separate nation state of Pakistan. While several different options of the nature of separate nations were discussed between 1945 and 1947, eventually political differences and widespread and systematic violence led the subcontinent into the most extreme of these options—that of two separate countries (Roy 2018).

Conclusion

The emergence of religion as the primordial, primary, and essential identity of the people of India was one of the most far-reaching consequences of modernity in the subcontinent. This one feature of our modernity has impacted several aspects of the public life of religion in the region, including its influential presence in the political life of the nations that emerged from the fiery cauldron of the partition of British India. Religion in contemporary South Asia does not merely indicate identity, it has also emerged prominently as the ground on which civilizational and cultural claims are staked, loyalties vetted, citizenships granted or rescinded, and histories inscribed. The modern transformation of religions in the Indian subcontinent has involved close dialogue with modern socio-religious movements, its contextualization within anti-colonial discourse, and its revitalization as a source of moral and spiritual communities. Thus religion in modern India is closely associated with the nation-state project, particularly its cultural nationalist aspects, in a manner that remains difficult to dislodge. When state technologies of data collection are added to this mix, the process of turning religion into identity and a civilizational marker is complete. Its long-term ramifications are still unfolding before us.

2

Religion as Practice

Religion is most commonly associated in our minds with religious texts and scriptures. These lay down philosophical and didactic aspects of each religion—especially the scriptural ones. Belief in the core teachings of the scriptures is widely understood to be the basis of a religious life. However, religion is often much more deeply connected with what people do—small and big acts that they participate in—than what they believe in. Belief is abstract. On the other hand, religious acts, at times based upon doctrine and at other times carried out as part of custom and tradition, are central to the lived religious worlds of a vast majority of people. Prayers, congregations, fasting, festivals, rites, rituals, pilgrimages, and acts of charity constitute what it means to be religious and express faith and piety.

Religion in India. Varuni Bhatia, Oxford University Press.
© Varuni Bhatia 2025. DOI: 10.1093/oso/9780198958345.003.0003

Anthropologists have for a long time been deeply invested in understanding and analysing the religious life worlds of ordinary people by turning to their material culture. Using ethnography as their primary means and method, anthropologists have tried to make sense of the practices, observances, everyday performances, and transformations within religious communities. Unlike their textually oriented colleagues, such as historians, philosophers, or theologians, anthropologists are interested in religion as a 'habitus' that informs and frames the embodied world of current and lived traditions. Religion is, in the words of one of the most important anthropologists of religion, a 'cultural system' that produces dispositions, creates communities, and establishes belief systems based on symbolic acts and their interpretation (Geertz 1966). The anthropological approach understands religions through material, immanent, and broad praxis–based concepts that exist across religious traditions. In the context of India, where the boundaries of scriptural or classical religion are being constantly pushed by its practised or lived aspects, focusing on how people lead religious lives and engage with the world around them in religiously informed ways is a significant aspect of understanding everyday religion. This chapter will look at 'popular' and 'everyday' religion through sacred space, ritual, and pilgrimage in India and tease out its intersections with secular modes of being.

Sacred Space and Ritual in Indian Religions

On National Highway 62, a few dozen kilometres from the tourist attraction of Jodhpur, stands an unusual shrine. The shrine consists of a raised platform upon which are placed several stone images, painted upon to resemble the face of a mustachioed man. A framed painting and photograph jostle for space on the same platform. Devotees throng to the site, circumambulating the platform, making offerings to the enshrined deity. Just outside the platform's periphery, small shops and vendors selling trinkets, toys, cheap cosmetics, flowers, and sweets line up. However, it is what lies behind the platform that makes this shrine truly unique. In a glass case stands a motorcycle—a 350 cc Royal Enfield Bullet. The same devotees who circumambulate the platform, pray before it, and receive blessings via the priest, also excitedly take selfies of themselves with the motorcycle in the background. The selfie-with-the-enshrined-motorcycle seems to be yet another mode of devotional ritual practice at the site, complementing the older, more recognizable ones of *puja* (ritual worship), *arti* (waving lamps before a deity), and *prasad* (receiving blessing from the deity in the form of flowers or food).

What makes this, and so many other spaces like it, sacred? Sacred spaces, to quote Arjun Appadurai, 'come in every size and scale, from small family shrines to village temples, to lineage temples, to regional temples, to great pan-regional pilgrimage centers' (Appadurai 1981: 8–9). Appadurai was speaking primarily about Hindu temples in Tamil Nadu, but his observation holds true of all kinds of sacred spaces everywhere in India. What separates a temple, a domestic shrine, a church, a dargah, a mosque, a gurdwara, from each other? Is it merely their religious affiliations? Do these spaces share more commonalities than differences? How is the 'size and scale' of a sacred place to be determined? What accounts for their continued significance, sometimes extending over centuries? Mircea Eliade, scholar of comparative religion, argued that sacred spaces mark the site of a hierophany or 'the act of manifestation of the sacred' (Eliade 1987: 11). God/s erupted or appeared there—or so the believers fervently believe. Eliade argues that sacred spaces are marked by both myth and ritual. Myth narrates the story of the 'original' eruption of the sacred at the given site while ritual ensures a cyclical repetition of the event of eruption.

Thus, for instance, the devotional songs associated with the shrine of 'Motorcycle Baba' Om Banna recount the unfortunate accident at that very spot on the highway that snatched away the life of its young rider, only to transform him into a spirit-deity who protects those who travel the same roads. In a more complex and historically much longer hierophanous vein, the legend of the Meenakshi Temple at Madurai recounts how the Pandya king who commissioned the earliest structure of the temple stumbled upon the already sacred site of the birth of the Goddess Meenakshi while hunting in a dense forest (Fuller 1992). Similar legends can be found around big and small temples across the subcontinent. Legends of the Kalighat Temple at Kolkata relate it as the site where a part of Sati's body (her foot or little finger, depending upon who you ask) fell. The annually occurring Urs celebrations at any dargah celebrate the divine union between the *pir* (the spiritual master) buried at the dargah and God. There is an orderly repetition of big and small acts of piety and devotion at sacred sites carried out by common devotees—from lighting incense to prayer and chanting. Thus, sacred space is ordered within a rationale of everyday repetitions, connected to a world of myth and legend, and regulated by praxis that sets these spaces apart from secular spaces—such as government offices—or public spaces—such as a bus terminal or a market.

Anthropologists of religion designate any space that is used for prayer, congregation, or religious ritual as a sacred space. While a domestic altar or shrine may share some of the characteristics of sacredness, a sacred space is also by definition a public space—although there can sometimes exist restrictions pertaining to who can enter and what must be worn when entering this space. In India, while sacred spaces are abundant, there are differences between different religious traditions as to what purpose a sacred space serves. For instance, Hindus regard a temple as a spatial manifestation of its presiding deity where ritual worship takes place in a regular and systematic fashion (Appadurai 1981). Muslims understand a mosque to be a congregational prayer hall that allows those praying therein to 'centre' and direct their prayers and dispensations. This takes place quite literally, because of the presence of the *qibla*, a niche in the west-facing wall, that points towards Mecca—the paradigmatic sacred space within Islam. A dargah on the other hand becomes sacred as a place where 'the power of the saint has been transferred to the land itself' (Bellamy 2011: 216). For the Sikhs, a gurdwara is as much a congregational prayer hall as a museum and a receptacle for a sacred object—the edition of the Guru Granth Sahib that lies within its precincts. Alongside the Sikh sacred text, a gurdwara may also host several other sacred objects such as swords or footwear or even a piece of clothing worn by one of the Sikh gurus. For Jains as well as Buddhists, sacred space is a place of meditation, and a place for the performance of certain penances and practices of meditation. Rituals are also a part of Buddhist and Jain reverence of exalted beings, such as bodhisattvas and *tirthankars* (lit., ford-maker). Depending upon its denomination, age, and use, a church may simply be a prayer hall or connote something more than that—such as a site of healing or the burial place of a significant member of the community. Thus, each religion understands sacred space in a different fashion.

And yet, for myriad believers who throng to sacred spaces as pilgrims, devotees, tourists, or the occasional curious onlooker, these spaces also carry shared characteristics, recognizably religious as well as secular. For a sacred space is a place of prayer, worship, service, and community. All spaces contain elements of veneration, authority, healing, charisma, ritual practice, and social collectives. Sacred spaces can also be spaces of power and exclusionary practices. These common features may have to do with the journeys undertaken to sacred sites (pilgrimage) by faithful devotees, the big and small acts of piety and charity that are carried out at these sites (prayer and rituals), the religious (and also secular) authorities

that variously administer the sacred sites, or the buzz-
ing commercial activity that often accompanies them.
These spaces are sites of what people do as much as
what they believe in. And it is not uncommon to find
identifiable local characteristics in different sacred
spaces and the practices that they enshrine. The
smell of incense and garlands; the offerings of cloth,
oil, food items, flowers, and a myriad of objects;
the sprinkling and consumption of holy liquids; the
mediating person between the devotee and the object
of their devotion; the jostling crowds trying to catch
a sight of the object of veneration enshrined therein;
secondary shrines or spaces around the main one; and
the thick air of hope and belief are some of the most
common features. One need not be a scholar of comparative religions to observe and experience these at
first hand, irrespective of the religious tradition one
may be dealing with.

Everyday religiosity in India is also very much a
domestic practice, in addition to being performed at
public sacred spaces. Scholars of gender and religion
have repeatedly commented upon the key role played
by ritual and piety in determining the everyday religious lives of women. In Hindu traditions, religious
rites and ritual inform women's domestic religiosities
in significant fashion. These are often characterized
by a combination of quotidian and festive rites, fasting

and feasting, and everyday acts of prayer and worship. These rites often serve to forge communities and strengthen kinship ties. In a typical Hindu context, domestic rites, *vrats* (vows) and *pujas* (worship), for the longevity of the male members of the family, for prosperity, for general well-being, or for getting rid of minor ill omens, are some of the key responsibilities that often fall on the shoulders of women. A vast majority of Muslim women in the subcontinent conduct their daily prayers (*namaz* or *salat*) within their homes often alongside other female members of the family, while the men congregate, especially for the Friday afternoon prayers, at a space designated for the same—often, this place is the *masjid*. The women are also responsible for training the younger members of the family in the correct performance of Muslim piety. For a vast majority of women in India, irrespective of their religious affiliation, religious practices are never divorced from their domestic responsibilities of caregiving as well as upholding the dignity and honour of the family. In a rapidly modernizing India, the performance of domestic rites and pietistic practices has not lost its significance despite often being criticized as being superstitious or moribund. Domestic rites and acts of piety have instead transformed into markers of status and prestige in an evolving urban, cosmopolitan, and aspirational context. As families and kinship networks disperse, new forms of media are innovatively used to assist the performance of these domestic rites and pietistic acts.

Place-Making in Local and Translocal Sacred Sites

In a five-kilometre radius of where I live in peri-urban Bangalore, there is a vast array of sacred spaces. Most of these are humble shrines, some barely have a stable or *pucca* structure and others are rough-cut stones placed under a tree and daubed with powder, dried flowers, and other such signs of worship. There are a few modest dargahs. In this vast and rapidly changing landscape from rural to urban, certain types of Hindu temples have been recently renovated. One, in particular, is representative of the transformations that urbanization and the substantial rise of a cosmopolitan, upwardly mobile, and largely privileged Hindu population in the neighbourhood have effected. Under a *peepal* tree stand three tall, oval-shaped stones. These, and many like them, are worshipped by the local population as aniconic representations of one or other *amman*, such as Yellamma or Mariamman—both very popular in southern India as wish-fulfilling and healing deities. Another rough shrine dedicated to the *navagrahas* (the nine planetary deities that purportedly control individual and family fortunes), and *nagadevatas* (serpent deities) existed behind this particular *peepal* tree. Over the last few years, a new, grand, and colourful temple with a tower has been constructed. And within this newly constructed temple, the image of *kodanda* Rama (Rama-with-a-Bow) has been consecrated. The platforms dedicated to the *navagrahas* and the *nagadevatas* have also received an upgrade by being brought within the precincts of this new Rama temple. The shrines to Yellamma and Mariamman, however, have been left outside with the bare minimum of upgrade.

Sacred spaces, Smriti Srinivas argues, are a manner of place-making—of adding meaning to otherwise strange, dangerous, or empty spaces. They are a way in which we relate to spaces through a mythic and ritualistic framework. However, they are not devoid of social contestations or historical pasts. In her study of Bangalore's sacred spaces, Srinivas draws attention to the manner in which older shrines and the customs around them continue to flourish, albeit in a repurposed fashion (Srinivas 2001). Sacred spaces often have an ecological component to them—as entire landscapes can be fenced off and declared sacred. It is not unusual in India to find rivers, lakes, trees, groves, and hills, either as extensions of an existing sacred site or designated as sacred in and of themselves. Across the nation, a careful observer may be able to discern a frenetic pace of renovation and upgrading of big and small Hindu temples, thereby assisting the (re)territorialization of space. As sacred spaces become larger, or more prominent, there is a bureaucratization of their care and management, often with the aim of modernizing them and 'cleaning them up'. Urban centres in India often enfold multiple sacred sites that are connected to the history of that particular city or town. In Bangalore, for example, the Dharmaraja Temple (the site of the city's annual *karaga* procession), the Sai Baba temples dotting the city, the shrines to the infant Jesus and Mary in working-class neighbourhoods, and the Basilica of St Mary in the colonial centre are key sacred sites that provide meaning and history to the city. These sites narrate the story of the emergence of the city and its transformations from the eighteenth to the twenty-first centuries.

A critical feature that characterizes certain sacred spaces in India is their close association with healing. As sites of healing, and of wish-fulfilment, several sacred sites also host a range of possession rituals as well as 'miracles'. Devotees, sometimes across religious affiliations, throng to shrines of wish-fulfilling and healing deities such as Shanidev, Mariamman, Sitala, or Hanuman to ask for blessings before an exam, or for good luck in a job interview, in marriage, and/or in childbirth. At the shrine of Nanhe Mian at Firoz Shah Kotla in Delhi, aspirants write petitionary notes asking for intervention in a difficult situation or protection against misfortune from the *pir* (Taneja 2018). The Basilica of Our Lady of Velankanni, also known as 'Lourdes of the East', is popular as a site of succour, protection, and healing. Her statues dot roadside shrines across towns and cities in southern India (Bloomer 2018). In many ways, then, sacred spaces are not merely spaces of order, but also sites where *disorder* and pathos are expressed, articulated, and even addressed. Gods, deities, and other powerful spirits are immanent in these spaces; they are answerable to their devotees there as some form of redressal platforms. These answers, more often than not, appear to believers in the form of miracles—impossible deeds and speech acts that have a salubrious and gainful end.

Anthropologists have tried to analyse the wide variety that we can observe between different sacred spaces through spatial-structural frameworks, such as 'local/popular/vernacular/folk' and 'pan-Indian/textual/classical' religion. Popular Hinduism revolves around village or 'folk' deities (*grama devata*) who respond, favourably or unfavourably, to ritual acts performed (or not performed) at their shrines. Deities of classical Hinduism, on the other hand, such as Vishnu or Shiva or one of the Puranic goddesses, are largely beyond the demands of everyday life and are mainly concerned with granting salvation or *moksha* (Babb 1975; Fuller 1992). Vernacular Islam refers to a host of practices of veneration, prayer, healing, and miracles that take place in the context of Sufi shrines and through faith-healers across the Indian subcontinent (Flueckiger 2006; Bellamy 2011). Local forms of Christianity in India participate in similar kinds of practices of healing, miracles, and possessions, accompanied by charismatic or saintly figures, veneration of Virgin Mary in her local manifestations and the saints (Dempsey 2001; Bloomer 2018). Pentecostal forms of Christianity while eschewing saint and Mary veneration, participate enthusiastically in collective forms of chanting and healing rituals. Practising and believing Jains often visit the shrines of major or minor or local deities to invoke their blessings on special occasions. Everyday religion in India often looks different from its classical or scriptural articulations. A careful observer will also be able to discern overlaps between locally-informed popular religious practices across religious traditions. Moreover, everyday religion is closely intertwined with other forms of quotidian life in India: urbanization and migration, the rise of a substantial and consuming middle class with its socio-economic anxieties, the bureaucratization of spaces and practices, claims of recognition, and questions of labour and work (Ibrahim 2024).

The spatial relationship between these local, quotidian forms of religious practices and classical religion is one of contestation and collaboration. Often these contestations and collaborations are worked out in a ritualistic fashion. Kancha Ilaiah has questioned the structural understanding of local deities as 'folk' or 'vernacular' variations of classical traditions, especially when it comes to Hinduism. He argues that these so-called local deities and the spaces and practices associated with them ought not to be considered as part of the larger Hindu world in any way. He argues that they are the material and immanent religious traditions of a vast majority of Indians, located in their everyday social, political, and economic struggles. The deities, too, are associated with agriculture and pastoralism, healing and nourishment, thereby forming a habitus independent of the salvation-granting and transcendental deities of classical Hinduism. Hence, non-classical deities and their devotees should be counted out of the larger Hindu fold (Ilaiah 1996). While several Hindu leaders vehemently oppose Ilaiah's interventions, they nevertheless throw down a significant challenge to how we understand the role of religion, especially Hinduism, in Indian society.

Sacred spaces are not bereft of power and conflict—in fact, quite the opposite. They have fundamentally been spaces of power, authority, and wealth. Legends around sacred spaces speak of them as sites of extreme purity, chastity, valour, healing, or miracles. Such legends only add to the immanent power that they embody. And not all sacred spaces are inclusive. Certain Hindu shrines such as Ayyappa Temple at Sabarimala and Shanidev Temple in Shingnapur disallowed women from entering the temple premises until recently. The Jagannath Temple at Puri customarily bars non-Hindus from entering. South Asian masjids are typically not open for women to offer prayers. Conversely, however, the dargah of a Sufi pir is for the most part open to receive visitors across religious and gender boundaries, while it is not unusual to find local Hindu devotees in a gurdwara or local Jain worshippers in local Hindu shrines. It is a feature of our present-day identity-driven understanding that when we think of contestations around sacred spaces, it is within the framework of interreligious conflict. However, there are multiple stakeholders within a sacred space, including secular authorities and constitutional law, and contestations are more often mundane than exceptional.

Every Thursday, throngs of devotees across religious affiliations gather at the shrine of Nanhe Miyan within the ruins of Firoz Shah Kotla. These devotees, many of whom are women, hail from the lower middle-class, working-class, and urban-poor neighbourhoods of Delhi. They leave petitionary letters in crevices and nooks of the ruins of the Kotla, hoping for a miracle. Nanhe Miyan is considered to be a *jinn*—a supernatural being in Islamic tradition capable of intervening on behalf of mortals. Curiously, though, any understanding of the supernatural powers of the place was non-existent prior to 1977. That is when devotees started to come to the place to ask for favours from the resident jinn. The shrine poses a triangular conflict, between its working-class and subaltern devotees who come here for succour and safety, the theological authorities of Islam who consider such practices to be a corrupted form of Islam, and the Archaeological Survey of India that wants to protect the medieval monument of Firoz Shah Kotla from its lived present (Taneja 2018).

Access to sacred space has been one of the most abiding contestations in the history of the subcontinent. It has taken several different kinds of legal measures to ensure equal access, especially with regard to Hindu sacred spaces. Early twentieth-century temple-entry movements mark a key process by which marginal and outcaste groups were able to gain access to orthodox Hindu temples. In the late nineteenth and early twentieth century, the princely state of Travancore (now within the state of Kerala) and parts of Madras Presidency (now the state of Tamil Nadu) witnessed some of the earliest temple-entry movements in modern India. The most significant of these movements was the Vaikom Satyagraha that started in 1924 and lasted for twenty months. It was a movement to allow Ezhavas and Pulayars of Travancore, who had been traditionally barred not only from entering prominent temples but also from using the streets and grounds around it, to access these spaces. Under inspiration from the followers of Sree Narayana Guru and SNDP Yogam, radical social reformer Ayyankali, and caste-Hindu members of the Kerala Congress, the movement was ultimately successful (Jefferey 1976). The Vaikom Satyagraha became the first of many such contestations that eventually led to the opening of Hindu religious spaces to all Hindus, irrespective of their caste.

Pilgrimage and Charity

Pilgrimage is a journey, often long and sometimes arduous, undertaken with a religious intent or purpose. Every religious tradition, both contemporary and in the past, has had significant pilgrimages that its faithful undertake. Scholars note that the study of pilgrimage entails understanding the place, the journey, and the people involved in it in a connected fashion. Anthropologists variously understand pilgrimage undertaken by devotees through the lens of community formation, as the performance of a significant life ritual and a repetition of original and/or significant events in the history of that religion. Others have remarked upon the transformative nature of such journeys, whether due to their purported ability to grant salvation or through the healing powers of the place of pilgrimage. Many historians remark on the gradual emergence of a pilgrimage site over time, through a combination of several factors including patronage, trade networks, and available infrastructure for travel. Others pay attention to the economic dimensions of pilgrimage sites, noting the nodal role these sites often play as centres of commerce.

For a devotee or believer, a pilgrimage is a deeply transformative journey, undertaken with a specific religious end and purpose. This purpose may be a salvific one, which is what brings many Hindus to Kashi or Haridwar. Or it may be less lofty but no less significant, such as the health and happiness of oneself or a loved one—which is what brings devotees to places such as the Amman Temple at Samayapuram. Or it may be to partake in the supernatural charisma, the *karamat* or *baraka*, of a holy figure that is most closely associated with the place—which is what brings devotees across religious affiliations to the dargah at Nizamuddin or of Muinuddin Chishti, better known as Garib Nawaz, at Ajmer. Pilgrimages are transformative—most pilgrimages are arduous journeys where individual capacities are pushed to their limits and beyond. The presence of physical discomfort is as central to the pilgrimage as the journey itself. At times, discomfort is guaranteed by the location of the pilgrimage site itself. At other times, and especially during festivals associated with the particular shrine, bodily pain is actively embraced through the performance of acts that push the limits of human endurance.

Whatever perspective we may privilege in our understanding of pilgrimage, the scholar's or the believer's, it is important to note that every religious tradition in India has some form of pilgrimage associated with it. Additionally, each religious tradition also has sacred sites that host pilgrims from near and far in the country. Sometimes, these sites enjoy a more local provenance, limited to a single linguistic region and community. At other times, their fame is spread all over the country, and even beyond. Hence, many Hindus consider the pilgrimage to a sacred centre like Varanasi/Kashi/Benares as sacred due to its salvation-granting properties. It is considered a *tirthasthana*, literally a 'ford' connecting this world with the next. Pilgrimage to the tombs and shrines of saints and venerated figures is a central aspect of practices of popular Catholicism and Islam. These journeys and sites are associated with powers of healing and wish-fulfilment. Pilgrimages such as the *hajj* are ways of memorializing the original journey undertaken by the Prophet himself.

In the village of Gudugu in Andhra Pradesh, the annual pilgrimage consists of devotees cutting across religious affiliations coming to the *pir-makanam* (the dargah or resting place) of the local Muslim saint who lies buried there. That is the story of the sacred space of Gudugu which comes alive every pilgrimage cycle during the month of Muharram. The pilgrims are local residents and their families who may now be living far away for reasons that have to do with livelihood (Mohammad 2013). Pilgrims to Gudugu come from Hindu as well as Muslim faiths, and this pilgrimage allows them to reassert their local belonging. If this pilgrimage, one of the largest local gatherings in the state, is about belonging, there are other pilgrimages that seek to produce a sacred landscape. The annual Varkari pilgrimage of Maharashtra seeks to do just that. Each year, *palkis* or consecrated palanquins carrying the image of one or other Marathi bhakti poet travel across the state of Maharashtra and north Karnataka to the temple of Vithoba at Pandharpur. The pilgrimage ties together people, language, memory, and history in a manner that allows for the emergence of a cultural-linguistic landscape as a unified whole—a form of place-making (Feldhaus 2003).

This crucial aspect of place- and space-making, with a strong sense of belonging, in the context of sacred space and its political usages was recognized most significantly by Vinayak Damodar Savarkar when he claimed that, due to the presence of a multitude of holy spaces associated with Hinduism, India was the 'holy land' (*punyabhumi*) of the Hindus. However, and in an exclusionary move, Savarkar also argued that the same could not be said for Muslims and Christians since their primary religious sites were located outside the Indian subcontinent. In making such claims, Savarkar misunderstood how pilgrimage, sacred space, and place-making work at any given moment in history. Not only are there multiple pilgrimage sites associated with each religion, but several pilgrimage sites and holy places—such as the dargah of Moinuddin Chishti at Ajmer, or the bascilica of Our Lady of Velankanni in Tamil Nadu, or that of Baba Ramdev in Rajasthan—draw devotees and faithful from across the spectrum of religions in India.

Popular religion often transcends strict religious boundaries and remains embedded within broader networks of exchange of ideas, material objects, and devotional metaphors.

Take, for example, the Ayyappa Temple in Sabarimala in the state of Kerala. This shrine has been in the news in recent years due to its policy of refusing access to women of menstruating age (10–50 years) from its precincts—a policy that was declared unconstitutional by the Supreme Court in a 2019 judgement. However, it must be noted that while the legends associated with Ayyappa at Sabarimala specifically excluded a certain demographic from offering prayers there, ironically these legends were inclusive of male Muslim devotees of the deity. Indeed, for the pilgrimage to be considered complete, the Hindu men who undertake it must pay obeisance at the shrine of Vavar, a Muslim *pir* whose shrine is located at the foot of the hill where the main shrine stands.

In a somewhat different vein—yet perhaps not so different—each year in the month of March devotees gather at the Dharmaraja Temple in Bangalore for the commencement of the *karaga* (literally, water-pot) festival. Here too, the primary actors of the *karaga* hail from subaltern groups that reside in the city—its erstwhile community of agriculturalists and horticulturalists who were slowly pushed to the margins as the city grew, first into a British cantonment town and later into a centre of heavy industry and more recently into the software capital of India. Versions of these water-bearing journeys, done by young men called *kanwar*, are undertaken in the month of July/ August in various parts of north and central India (Singh 2017). The north Indian version of the *kanwariya* pilgrimage, where young men from regions as far-flung as Rajasthan, Haryana, Madhya Pradesh, and Chattisgarh walk by foot to Haridwar to collect the water of the Ganga river and walk back home with the holy water in pots, has emerged as one of the largest annual pilgrimages to take place in India. The respective state governments make extensive arrangements for the pilgrims, even though there are disruptions caused by hundreds of thousands of pilgrims walking on the highways.

Historically, pilgrimage networks have also been central to economic activity, and this continues to be the case in the present. Pilgrimage sites often dotted premodern trade routes and were the conduit of substantial movement of goods and people over history. Often these crucial aspects of trade, financial transactions, military movement, and migration are overlooked in studies that tend to focus primarily on questions of ritual function, community formation, place-making, and identities in the context of pilgrimages. The seventh-century Chinese Buddhist pilgrim Xuanzang (Hiuen Tsang) traversed significant portions of the Silk Route in his journey to India to discover Buddhist scriptures unavailable in his own country. Similarly, the hajj pilgrimage undertaken in seventeenth–eighteenth-century India was a crucial aspect of Mughal trade relations between the western coast of the subcontinent and the Arab peninsula. Mughal ships that sailed these seas, including carriers of pilgrims, were also key trading vessels between the subcontinent and its Arab neighbours. Pilgrimages and pilgrims did not just serve as active agents of transnational trade, they have historically been significant agents of subcontinental trade as well. Vaishnava ascetics, the *gosain* or the *bairagi*, were well-known traders, traversing the famous internal pilgrimage routes associated with sites of Vaishnava veneration, from Haridwar to Ujjain and Ayodhya, in the early modern period.

Today, as pilgrimage and religious tourism go hand in hand, we see the transformation of significant pilgrimage sites and sacred spaces into tourism hubs and conduits. This has, in turn, led to the significant rise in temple upgrade and management, including of well-known temples such as the Kashi Vishwanath. Economic activity tends to be high at pilgrimage centres, with markets, accommodation and food of various kinds, and other subsidiary commercial activities taking centre stage. In her study of religious spaces and organizations, Sriya Iyer finds that they provide a range of services that can be classified as both religious and secular (Iyer 2018). Religious activities include all forms of faith-based and faith-inducing activities, such as prayer, worship, and religious instruction. However, what social scientists like Iyer find fascinating are the secular dimensions that these sites and organizations are able to tap into. These include education, health, charitable acts, philanthropic programmes, and other such activities that assist the overall engagement that devotees can have with the said site or organization.

In fact, charity and philanthropy form a key feature of the religious lives of several Indians, and are often covered under various forms of *seva* (service) for Jains, Sikhs, and Hindus, and as *zakat* (charitable acts) for Muslims. While not directly associated with a sacred site, these acts of service and charity often provide a key dimension of the manner in which ordinary Indians imagine themselves to be religious actors. Sikh gurdwaras accept *seva* of pious Sikhs on a daily basis through their contribution to the *langar* or community kitchens. Pious Muslims regularly contribute a portion of their income towards charity, which often leads to the funding of schools, hospitals, or orphanages. India boasts a very large number of religious organizations and trusts that receive donations from people in order to manage and finance the upkeep of religious places as well as to undertake charitable acts. It is very common for religio-cultural organizations such as the Rashtriya Swayamsevak Sangh (RSS) to provide humanitarian service, often performed with a religious intent by individuals, during time of natural and other disasters. Such examples urge us to reconsider the relationship between philanthropy, charity, and religion as well as between the secular state and religious organizations (Bhattacharjee 2019).

Conclusion

Religion is not merely what people believe in, but also what they practise. Practised aspects of religion that include acts, spaces, substances, economies, and the contestations and collaborations over all of these, are as significant as its philosophical or doctrinal aspects —if not more so—to understanding religion in India. Seeing religion as lived practice, as a part of the habitus, allows us to step beyond the question of belief and transcendence to pay attention to the material and immanent aspects that make people into religious actors. And often, religious actors are simultaneously actors in other ways—as professionals, workers, philanthropists, healers, community leaders, citizens, teachers, and so on. Understanding religion as habitus of these actors makes it into a broader concept than a narrowly defined one founded on belief systems.

3

Caste, Sect, and Religion

Most of us today find ourselves framed by a configu-
ration of identities that states and societies co-produce
and perpetuate under different conditions of coercion
and consent. However, in their social presentation,
identities are often made to seem timeless, primordial, and organic. Religion, nationality, class, gender,
language, ethnicity, and race are key social structures that determine social, economic, and political
relations in most parts of the world while operating
as salient categories of identity. They conceal their
historicity and appear to be natural. It is important to
acknowledge, at the outset, that the naturalness and
organicity of social identities is heavily dependent
upon the manner in which these have been selectively
adopted by modern nation states to govern their populations (Dirks 2001). That said, in the context of

Religion in India. Varuni Bhatia, Oxford University Press.
© Varuni Bhatia 2025. DOI: 10.1093/oso/9780198958345.003.0004

India, there exists what is a uniquely Indian form of social identification and stratification—that of caste. The intersections between caste and religion in India are several and run deep. So much so that, at times in everyday parlance, the term used to denote one can also signify the other. Take, for instance, this song attributed to the nineteenth-century Bengali mystic and singer Lalon Fakir: *jat gelo jat gelo bole, ei ki ajob karkhana* ('you have lost your caste/religion, they say—what a confounded world this is!'). In Lalon's life and poetry, the term *jat* refers to both caste and religion. For according to legend, he, like his intellectual predecessor Kabir, was born a Hindu and a Vaishnava, but was tended to by a Muslim family after a bout of illness. This involuntary act of crossing social boundaries caused him to lose his birth identity—literally, his *jat*. Indeed, losing one's caste has been a fraught process by most accounts—one that effectively covers the arc from salvation to discrimination and even emancipation, from the theological to the political and social.

More recently, the question of caste and its relationship to religion has once again emerged as a moot point. The Supreme Court of India has been hearing petitions to grant the status of Scheduled Castes to marginalized groups of Muslims and Christians. This would allow Pasmanda Muslims and Dalit Christians to avail of the benefits of reservations thereby bringing them within the purview of affirmative action measures in India. This has thrown up a plethora of questions. Can members of doctrinally egalitarian Abrahamic faiths, such as Christianity and Islam, reasonably lay claim to a Dalit identity? What of the experience of untouchability as a uniquely Hindu religious expression that determines caste inequality? There is no gainsaying that caste is one, if not the primary structural contradiction in Indian society. e It rests on a historically sedimented yet entirely arbitrary hierarchy of birth-based social privileges and exclusions. Nonetheless, it has been notoriously slippery to define. Hence, a nuanced understanding of caste and religion is imperative in our times in order to uncover the intricate intersections between the two. Religion plays an important role in establishing, regulating, and, at times, even challenging caste-based social stratifications, hierarchies, and identities in India. Religious and caste identities operate within a similar framework of social exclusions and hierarchies to such an extent that at times it is difficult to tell one from the other. Oftentimes, these social inclusions and exclusions are inscribed on the bodies of the women of various caste and religious groups. While contemporary egalitarian and emancipatory movements relating to caste and gender are strongly embedded within a language of rights, in the long history of the subcontinent these have been articulated predominantly in the language of religion.

Caste, *Varna*, and Religion

Scholars have used several frameworks to understand caste. Tradition, culture, hierarchy, reciprocity, difference, separation, segregation, discrimination, marginality, backwardness, power, domination, and inequality are some of these broad conceptual frameworks. However, the predominant understanding of caste hinges upon the twin pillars of endogamy and inter-dining that, in turn, stand upon the foundations of purity and pollution that define Hinduism. While this definition of caste today is commonsensical as well as one that drives policy and politics, its exclusive location within Hindu orthopraxy, i.e. the Hindu ritual practice deriving from its scriptural injunctions, has more recently been questioned by contemporary scholars as well as proponents of Dalit Muslim and Dalit Christian equity (Ansari 2023). To discern contemporary debates, it is important to comprehend the pre-colonial and colonial history of *varna*, *jati*, and caste in India, including the close engagement between caste and religion.

The origins and features of caste have been analysed differently by scholars from different disciplinary orientations. Moreover, caste appears to operate differently, depending upon whether we assume a text-based or a field-based approach (Jodhka 2012). While there exists broad agreement regarding contemporary features of caste society, the question of origins, especially its nestling within Hindu religion, has remained a contentious one. This is due to two reasons. The first is a methodological one where the sources and approaches used to understand caste differ greatly within different disciplines; the second is the history of the study of caste itself, which is mired within the complex developments of the colonial state, its epistemological orientation, and anti-colonial movements in India. Irrespective of how we define and understand caste, its intersection with religion in contemporary India, and in the past, throws up unique perspectives that urge us to think of these two identities as not distinct but complementary to each other in remarkable ways.

Extant scholarship on caste, and its intersection with religion, can be divided into three disciplinary frameworks: the Indological, the historical, and the sociological-anthropological. The term *casta*, which later became 'caste', was first used by Portuguese seafarers to describe social groupings in western India (Guha 2013). It was only in the colonial period that

caste was systematically recognized as the basic structure of Indian society by state authorities. Amongst
the earliest writers to draw attention to caste as the
organizing principle of Indian society were British
scholar-administrators from the late eighteenth and
early nineteenth centuries who turned to Sanskrit
texts to grasp the vast and complex social world that
they observed around them. They understood caste
exclusively through the lens of Hindu scriptures.
But the ethnologists, administrators, and colonial
bureaucrats of later decades found scarcely any overlap between the fourfold order of the Hindu texts
and lived realities that they faced. In its perplexing
plurality, regional forms of social stratification defied
the structure and hierarchies of the categories of
Hindu classical texts. The colonial state nonetheless
proceeded to collect census data based upon caste
and religion in its decennial census and continued to
locate the origins of caste society in the scripturally
sanctioned *varna* (class–status) and *ashrama* (life-stage)
system of classical Hindu texts. This analysis of caste
society and its origins in religious scriptures continues to inform politics of emancipation and debates
around redistribution and justice into the present.

Indologists and textualists locate the origins of
caste society in the *varnashrama* stipulations of Hindu
religious texts. The Sanskrit scriptural term we most

commonly associate with caste is *varna*. *Varna* is a Sanskrit term that can variously mean colour, category, or genus. The Hindu legal texts and texts of polity such as the *Dharmashastras* and *Nitishastras* regularly speak of *varnashrama dharma* (duties based upon one's *varna* and *ashrama* status) as the basis of a lawful or dharmic society. One's *varna* in a given birth, according to Hindu scriptures, was determined by one's *karma* or deeds in the previous birth. And thus *dharma*, *karma*, and *varna* are established as the triad of socially normative and theologically determined concepts. The Hindu law books, scholars point out, are fairly clear regarding the rules of separation of varnas, as well as the hierarchical status of different varnas. According to Hindu law books and their authors such as Manu, Medhatithi, and Gautama, the basis of a 'lawful' or 'righteous' society was one where the four varnas would have settled and found a home (Aktor 2018). These texts demonstrate a considerable apprehension of the mixing of varnas, or marriages across different varnas. While *anuloma* marriages between an upper varna man and a lower varna woman were tolerated in these texts, the opposite *pratiloma* marriages resulted in the birth of outcastes. Law compendiums like the *Dharmashastras* lay down rules of occupation, rites, and rituals based upon the varna of the person. These included not only who could perform Vedic sacrifices, but also who could perform what kind of work. Thus, the world of Vedic sacrifice, which included taking an agentic role in religious rites, was reserved for the *dvija* or twice-born Brahmin, Kshatriya, and Vaishya—the priestly class, the warrior class, and the mercantile class, respectively—while those belonging to the remaining fourth class of Shudras—the servants or serving class—were merely the passive recipients of Vedic rites and rituals. This exclusion from active participation in Vedic rituals, according to law books, forms the basis of all the remaining exclusions and stratifications (Aktor 2018).

This, then, was the ideal and normative social world produced and reproduced endlessly in Hindu texts on appropriate social behaviour. Epics repeated the moral, ritual, and social righteousness of this order, and popularized them as ideal types. That a digression from varna-inscribed duties and occupation was considered disdainful can be discerned from a series of examples from the epics—from Krishna's teachings to Arjuna to Manduka's asceticism. The texts reproduce a world of Brahmin–Kshatriya hegemony and they do so with little or no reflection of the changing historical contexts within which they are composed. Hence, a series of regionally significant law compendiums and commentaries produced in Maharashtra between the twelfth and seventeenth centuries, for instance, show little concern for the historical transformations that emerge out of this crucial period when land and labour relations were undergoing dramatic changes. The only concession made by texts towards social reality is through the category of *apad dharma*, to be followed during times of expediency (Vajpeyi 2010).

Historians of caste, on the other hand, find themselves turning to political economy, land and commerce, and relationship to the court as determining factors of a hierarchically ordered and status driven caste society in India. While accepting the significance of the *Dharmashastras* in laying down the conditions of an ideal society, several historians point to the lack of any material evidence to prove a strict adherence to varna-based social order. Historians tend to understand social stratifications within frameworks of rank and status, particularly from the source-rich medieval and early modern period. Sumit Guha, in particular, analyses caste society in early modern India through the intersections of what he calls 'state power' and 'ethnic rank' which produces an ethnically determined, ranked society with a strict adherence to boundary-making. Here ritual status, socio-economic power, occupational guilds, kinship, and marriage all play determinative roles. In the sixteenth century what the Portuguese identified as castes were largely 'strong local organizations of councils of dominant peasants or tribes that controlled the countryside' that contributed to the creation of a 'supra local gentry' able to lay claim over, and appropriate, state resources (Guha 2013: 16). These ethnic groups operated at the intersections of their connections with courtly culture and state power: their ability to collect, distribute, and, at times, hold on to land revenue, as well as their control over commercial activities in their regions. Guha points to the relative absence of the terms *jat* or *jati* as well as *varna* in the land records, inscriptions, and other administrative records of medieval and early modern states in western India. Instead, he notes that the more prevalent terms were *quam* and *qabileh*, and these were used for closed social groups irrespective of their religious affiliations. As late as the end of the nineteenth century, *quam* was the term used in western princely states to denote what we would today broadly identify as kinship-based groups, such as the Rajputs. In effect, these dominant groups formed the 'little kingdoms' of the early modern period, defined by their competition and collaboration with the large and powerful players—be that the behemoth of the Mughal state or the uppity European trading companies that would soon change the rules of the game of power in the subcontinent.

What role does religion play, one may ask, in this historically informed and dynamic understanding of caste? Historical texture does point towards a displacement of structures of purity and pollution as determinants of caste hierarchy in favour of land relations. However, it recognizes the purity–pollution dyad as one among several other strategies of exclusions and boundary-making adopted by social groups. Ritual here does not exist beyond political economy but is, in fact, closely aligned with it. Hence, the processes of boundary-marking remain peculiarly tied to religious expressions. Who could enter which part of a temple? Who could worship which deity, or which manifestation of a deity? Who could engage what kind of ritual intermediary? While being articulated in ritual and religious language, these markers of boundary-making, and hence graded exclusions, were embedded in processes of state formation, military labour, and commercial activities as much as in scriptural sanctions in pre-colonial India.

Even as historians understand caste to be an outcome of dynamic transformations of state and society in South Asia, sociologists studying caste often take a more structuralist approach, looking for long-lasting and deep-rooted structural basis and justifications of current social realities. Early sociologists from India identified segmentation, hierarchy, restriction on social interaction, occupation, and marriage as the key characteristics of caste, with its 'purest form' being present within Hindu society. Louis Dumont in his landmark and influential *Homo Hierarchicus* (1970) argued that caste was fundamentally about hierarchy; it was a Hindu institution; and it had nothing to do with economic status or power. Instead, this hierarchy was based upon the principle of the opposition between pure and impure—with the Brahmin and the untouchable lying on the two ends of the extreme. Assessing Dumont's contribution to understanding caste in India, Surinder Jodhka notes that 'Dumont's book on the Indian caste system has perhaps been the single most influential academic work on the subject' (Jodhka 2012: 19). More than any other scholar, it was Dumont who provided us with an ideal type of caste society, laying bare the underlying structures of caste, without allowing the everyday or ordinary practices of caste relations that we may see around us to mar its structural neatness.

A vast range of anthropologically informed studies have challenged Dumont's ideal-type approach towards caste and offered insights into the various ways in which caste relations operate at a local and experiential level. M. N. Srinivas was one of the earliest Indian social anthropologists to counter the textual and idealized understanding of caste that we can see in Dumont's work. 'They have tried to perceive the complex facts of the caste system in terms of *varna*. This has resulted in a view of the structure which is ridiculously over-simplified,' he says, critiquing the textualist approach (Srinivas 1962:7). Srinivas contended that a study of caste in its operational form also shows that caste is dynamic and changing, not a stratified phenomenon. He recognized that entire castes could change their social rank and standing by using the twin processes of what he termed Sanskritization and Westernization.

Following Srinivas, sociologists in contemporary India have paid extensive attention to understanding caste through the lens of power and domination, the spread of democratic politics and privileges, and the emergence of a new political moment. In field-driven sociological scholarship, the question of power and domination emerged as central, with domination being mapped as much on to ritual as political economy, control over resources, and, more recently, education and employment. The role of the colonial and postcolonial state in caste enumeration, the *jajmani* system of exchange and mutuality, the relationship to land and means of production in rural India have continued to inform how caste operates. In contemporary India, caste has emerged as the fulcrum of democratic politics and a key ground over which questions of marginalization, redistribution, equity, and, perhaps most importantly, dignity are debated and resolved. And in several such instances of the contemporary public life of caste, religion is never far behind. It emerges as a particularly fecund question in the face of proclamations of the uniformity and egalitarian nature of various religious traditions.

Caste, Sect, and the Figure of the Guru

The figure of the religious master or preceptor, the *guru*, is one of the least studied aspects of Indian religious traditions, even though it is an extremely significant one. The guru shares several aspects with more conventional forms of religious authority, such as the priest or the legal expert. However, what differentiates a guru is the strong presence of the kind of charismatic authority that Max Weber first articulated in his works. According to Weber, one can locate three kinds of authorities—legal (state, the Constitution, and so on), traditional (community elders, ritual experts), and charismatic. The last is infused with a sense of being touched by the supernatural and is often seen to be boundless and beyond reason. This allows for a suspension of rational judgement and the inculcation of deep faith amongst their followers. One of the followers of Suraj Pal alias Bhole Baba, at whose *satsang* (congregation) in Hathras district in

July 2024, over a hundred people—mostly women from the most disadvantaged communities in Uttar Pradesh—lost their lives in a stampede, encapsulates this charisma most pointedly. As the bodies of the women who had died lay on the ground, he told a news reporter: 'Like you can only feel hunger, but cannot see it, you can only experience the power of Bhole Baba. You cannot see his magic, but you can feel it' (Pandey and Mishra 2024).

One of the more abiding frameworks that Louis Dumont gave to the study of religion and social stratification in India was that of the householder versus the renouncer. Dumont was not the first—nor was he the last—scholar to locate yet another fundamental dichotomy within Hinduism other than purity and pollution. The renouncer was 'Indian civilization's greatest creative force, a spectator, discoverer, and an innovator of India's great soteriologies' (Babb 2006: 224). The idealized figure of a charismatic renouncer able to challenge the deep, hierarchical structures of Indian society has been both a popular and a scholarly fascination in the Indian context. At times this individual is a renunciant, at other times a mystic, and at yet other times a storyteller and a prophet. Whatever may be the role, some characteristics hold this charismatic figure together, the key to which is the ability to collect a community of followers who believe that this person possesses charismatic authority. Often, such charismatic figures are able to leave behind them a succession of preachers, who continue to lead the community that identifies itself with the preceptors' name. This is what Weber has called the 'routinization of charisma' and the bureaucratization of its revolutionary aspects.

In his essay on sects in Indian religions, Lawrence Babb notes that while the meaning of 'sect' in English—as a breakaway group from the Church—does not quite apply to the Indian context, it has long been used by writers and scholars to denote what we many variously identify through indigenous terms such as *sampradaya*, *panth*, or *guru parampara* (Babb 2006). And in many ways, these so-called sectarian affiliations determine how popular religion is practised in India. What contemporary scholars identify as sects can be traced back to a long history of various kinds of religious traditions, cutting across modern-day religious identities, of a genealogically driven allegiance to a legendary or historical charismatic figure. Sometimes called the *sant* tradition, at other times identified with the bhakti movement, and at yet other times identified with the *shramana* or renouncer traditions of the early Indian past, these genealogically defined communities attribute central importance to the figure of a spiritual preceptor who grants a vision of salvation and emancipation—spiritual as well as social—and forges a congregational community.

Scholars have analysed the groups of followers, both householder and monastic, that emerge from these charismatic guru figures as key sources of resistance to Hinduism's inherent social stratifications. They variously push the boundaries of ritual and purity, extend their membership to a broader social class, and make allegiance to a guru, rather than birth, the primary marker of belonging. There is a long history of what we can characterize as religious sects—from the Kapalikas and Kalamukhas, Aghoris, Siddhas, and Virashaivas to Nath Panthis, Nanak Panthis, Kabir Panthis, and Bauls. While these sects should be considered 'Indic' due to their adherence to theories of karma and rebirth, it is also important to bear in mind that several of them held doctrinal positions that opposed Hindu orthopraxy. In recent times, however, sects have operated as closed groups, akin to kinship-based communities. And while the principle of descent was in theory cut loose from its location in birth, sects were able to turn into caste-like formations over a period of time. In several cases, preceptors cater to a specific kinship group that then turns into a sect that is also driven by caste regulations. We can see an example of this kind of emergence of caste-based sectarian tradition amongst the Namashudras of Bengal from the early nineteenth century. Under the charismatic leadership of Ramsharan Pal, the Matua community was forged, gaining recognition as a sect or a *sampradaya* of Bengali Vaishnavism, a 'deviant' one according to orthodox commentators. Under the influence of prominent modern-day leaders such as Jogendranath Mandal, what began as a religious movement also assumed secular and liberatory dimensions that spoke of issues of political representation, redistribution of resources, and dignity (Bandyopadhyay 2004).

Scholars usually trace two kinds of distinctions within these so-called sectarian Indic traditions: the *nirgun* and *sagun* types. *Nirgun* tradition considers divine to be beyond physical manifestations, and locates its expression in sound itself, which is transmitted as esoteric or mystical knowledge from a guru to a disciple through the granting of the sacred word. There is no better example to understand the key role played by the guru than Sikhism—a religion that holds discipleship or teaching, literally *sikhi*, at its doctrinal core and praxis. The life of the first Sikh guru, Nanak, as told and retold in various Sikh biographical literatures of *janamsakhis* and *vars*, recounts several tropes of superhuman greatness that we find in the biographies of other great figures and founders of religions, such as the Buddha and Prophet Muhammad.

Nanak was born into an upper caste and reputed family in the Punjab region. However, his attention soon turned away from the family profession of accounting and mercantilism to spirituality and mysticism. During one of his many wanderings, he got lost, and was presumed to have drowned in the river. However, inside the waters, he heard a divine voice telling him that there is one god, who is formless and can be understood only by the grace of the guru. This became the core teaching that Nanak, now a prophet, disseminated amongst his followers and disciples. His teaching marks the beginning of the Sikh sacred scripture and is recited as the *Japji* amongst Sikh congregations today. Nanak turned into a wandering prophet after receiving the teaching, and gathered around him a band of followers, both Hindu and Muslim. Nanak's legends refer to his several interactions with representatives of contemporaneous religious orders, from orthodox Muslim authorities to the Hindu yogis and practitioners of various austerities and rituals. However, the legends show Nanak to have the upper hand in each one of these interactions, thereby demonstrating the limitations of ritualistic or excessively rule-bound practices of religion—such as offerings and pilgrimages.

As the first guru of the Sikhs, Nanak establishes a succession of gurus, which continues up until the tenth one, Guru Gobind Singh. In the intervening century and a half, between the first and the last, the Sikhs conjoin spiritual and temporal authority in the figure of the guru, turning him simultaneously into a teacher and a warrior, a spiritual preceptor and an earthly king. The followers of the Sikh gurus were able to cohere as an initiated group called *Khalsa* (literally, pure), which later became the basis of an exclusive Sikh identity that coalesced in the colonial period. Historians have noted how, under the leadership of Guru Gobind Singh, a large number of Jat agriculturalists in the Punjab region became Sikh, sporting the identifying markers of unshorn hair, the sword, the iron bangle, the turban, and shorts. Despite their unique identity and history, the Sikhs were not recognized as a separate religion in colonial census records until the early twentieth century, when, due to the efforts of Sikh reform movements, they were able to stake a claim to be considered as a separate world religion and not merely as a sect within Hinduism.

In this context, it is also worth recalling the various *panth* traditions that failed to do so. Kabir Panth and Dadu Panth are two such traditions that remained within the broad umbrella of Hinduism as it evolved in the late nineteenth century, encompassing a vast number of sects and groups. What is also perhaps equally important to bear in mind is that while a vast majority of Sikhs gradually embraced a *Khalsa* organizational identity, some sections continued to accept the validity of 'living gurus' who traced their genealogy from Guru Nanak himself. In Punjab and other parts of north-western India, these 'living gurus' are often able to attract followers from a range of marginalized castes. Organized as *deras*—a term now used for religious collectives but used in the past to denote the military camps of the Mughal era— these religious collectives or sects often articulate a critique of caste hierarchies in their local and religious contexts (Ram 2007).

Caste and Resistance through Religion

Gail Omvedt, scholar of anti-caste movements in modern India, argues in her book *Seeking Begumpura* that one can discern a genealogy of anti-caste intellectuals in India, starting with the Buddha himself, who have been religious preachers. Omvedt places the medieval bhakti poets, especially those from the Marathi Varkari Nath Yogi, and north Indian *sant* traditions—such as Kabir, Nanak, and Ravidas—in this genealogy of anti-caste intellectuals and religious preachers in India (Omvedt 2008). Her book is a landmark in bringing together religion and an indigenous emancipatory discourse wherein the language of religion holds within itself a kind of a social revolution. If *varna* is understood as a uniquely Indian form of social structure and hierarchy whose roots are to be found in Hindu scriptures, it is not improbable to find challenges to the same within alternative religious movements from within the subcontinent. This was the basis of Dr Ambedkar's interest in Buddhism which he saw as the only religion appropriate for humanists and rationalists (Ambedkar 2011). For while he was not the first intellectual of modern India to locate an anti-caste philosophy in Buddhist teachings, he certainly was the most prominent and consequential one to inaugurate a public movement around it. In 1956, one year before his death, and after several decades of deep engagement with Buddhism, Dr Ambedkar formally took *diksha* (initiation) into Buddhism at a public event attended by thousands of people. Over the decades, hundreds of thousands of Dalit all over India have embraced Navayana Buddhism as a religion that is free from the structures of caste—an edifice that contemporary Indian Buddhists hold to be the basic characteristic of

Hindu religion. Dr Ambedkar's emancipatory vision and his interpretation of the Buddha's teachings loom large over this religious praxis.

Let us return to the argument made by Gail Omvedt to unearth what is, perhaps, one of the more vexed and unanswered questions of Indian religious history. What happened to Buddhism in the Indian subcontinent? How and why did it 'disappear' so suddenly? While there cannot be a straightforward answer to these questions that adequately addresses all the historical complexities, there is enough evidence from various linguistic and regional traditions of the subcontinent to argue that Buddhism did not in fact 'disappear' but became a part of the pluralistic religious life world of early to late medieval India. We find an increasing presence of Buddhist metaphysics and themes in the poetry and praxis of the Siddhas in southern India and the Nath *sampradaya* in north India. Renouncer traditions continue to flourish and casteless renouncers remain powerful figures. By the early centuries of the medieval period, this pluralistic religious world resulted in an effusion of poets and poetry all over the subcontinent—the Mahanubhavas, Varkaris, Siddhas, Nath Panthis, and Sahajiyas are some of the religious traditions where key concepts of Buddhist metaphysics and praxis became intertwined with the lived experiences of ordinary people, people from peasant and artisanal communities, creating a remarkable poetry of emancipation and salvation simultaneously.

On the one hand, while Buddhism and later Buddhist-informed religious traditions continued to inform resistance against centuries of caste-based exclusion and discrimination in the Indian subcontinent, caste-like structures were also beginning to seep into structurally egalitarian religions that came into the region and became more and more indigenized. Hence, over the same period that the bhakti revolution was sweeping through the region, we see rank and status society impact the lives of Muslims in India—ordinary people as well as the nobility. Imtiaz Ahmad is one of India's pioneer sociologists who has proposed that caste—or, at the very least, caste-*like* structures—existed within Indian Muslim communities (Ahmad 1978). Ahmad concluded that 'the system of social stratification among the Muslim communities ... is certainly comparable to the Hindu caste system though an exact parallel between them cannot be said to exist' (Ahmad 1978: 4). He goes on to argue that amongst the five key characteristics of Hindu caste society as noted by sociologists and anthropologists, four exist in variegated forms amongst Muslims in India. These are endogamy, occupational specialization, hierarchical ordering, and restrictions on social intercourse and commensality (Ahmad 1978). However, the key missing link is the religious justification for caste—an ideological construct based on the binaries of purity and pollution that we have discussed earlier in this chapter.

In recent months, debates over caste in Islam and Christianity have emerged as pressing policy concerns relating to the extension of reservations to Dalit Muslim and Dalit Christian communities. There are those who argue that caste, especially caste discrimination, is an exclusively Hindu phenomenon. However, scholars working on Dalit Christian communities and colonial and contemporary India have argued that discrimination continues to remain a key aspect of their everyday lived experience (Viswanath 2014). In the context of Islam, Shireen Azam shows that not only do caste-like divisions exist amongst Indian Muslims, they are also systematically upheld by theological commentators and lived practices amongst them (Azam 2023). She asserts that while a majority of India's Muslims are converts from indigenous populations, and the act of conversion (even to a purportedly egalitarian religion, in principle) does not change the caste status of the converts. She refers to several studies that have been done in the past to show that the distinction between *Ajlaf* and

Ashraf continues to be a significant one in every-day Muslim practice in India and is cemented in fatwas and socio-legal texts composed by Muslim reformers and modernizers from the colonial period (Azam 2023).

Ahmad's proposition, to recognize caste in Islam, and Azam's painstaking parsing-out of how caste discrimination operates both theologically and in social practice, and Viswanath's analysis of the political economic conditions of 'pariah' Christians during the colonial period invite us to rethink the question of caste in India, especially as it is reduced to being an essentially Hindu one. They also compel us to revisit the assumption of religious uniformity as well as the burden of minority that is attributed to the Muslim (or, for that matter, Christian) figure in contemporary India (Ansari 2023). They bring together ritual hierarchy, hierarchy of rank and status, and political economy considerations to offer a larger and more significant insight—that caste and religion operate as overlapping and often indistinguishable forms of separation, segregation, hierarchization, and discrimination. Caste and religion cannot be seen as clean and separate sociological entities and instead operate at the intersection with each other. This is what Lalon Fakir, with whom we began this chapter, understood quite well.

Conclusion

A clean separation between caste and religion, and the role that these play in determining social relations in contemporary India, is detrimental to a comprehensive analysis of both. In the current context, when the demand for recognition, representation, and equitable distribution of resources is key, the questions of marginalization and minoritization cannot be understood separately from each other. In contemporary India, caste bears the burden of marginalization and the disadvantage associated with it, while religion bears the burden of minoritization and the invisibility (or, alternately, hyper-visibility) associated with it. However, it is only when these two aspects are understood as two sides of the same coin of inequality that we can discern how caste and religion operate very much in tandem with each other as social institutions and identities.

4

Law and Religion

What is the nature of the relationship between religion and law—in India and elsewhere in the world?
Perhaps we may want to direct that question to the
interfaith couple denied protection from their relatives by the Allahabad High Court to pursue a live-in
relationship on the basis of such relationships being
disallowed within Islamic law (Ahsan 2024). The
hijab ban, the Uniform Civil Code debates, the crim-
inalization of Triple Talaq, the entry controversy at
the Ayyappa Temple in Sabarimala, and many other
such flashpoints in contemporary India demonstrate
beyond doubt the intense intertwining of law and
religion. However, in commonsensical as well as academic understanding of religion, while faith, belief,
ritual, sacred space, scripture, and community appear
most often as keywords, very rarely, if ever, does law

Religion in India. Varuni Bhatia, Oxford University Press.
© Varuni Bhatia 2025. DOI: 10.1093/oso/9780198958345.003.0005

feature on the same list. Given the critical role played by law and the courts in determining several aspects of religious practices, identities, and core teachings in contemporary India, it would create a major lacuna to ignore this. Moreover, religious law has been a key feature of the praxis and doctrinal systems of several of the world religions throughout history. The relationship between law and religion has surfaced as a particularly intimate one globally in the last couple of centuries with the emergence of secularism as an important and much-debated political tenet.

Law, Secularism, and the Indian Constitution

Secularism has been constitutionally adopted as a fundamental principle of the state and polity by several modern nation-states, including India. The term 'secular' was added to the Preamble of the Indian Constitution through the 42nd Amendment in 1976. However, it would not be accurate to say that India was a non-secular or religious country prior to the insertion of the term in the Preamble. At the moment of Independence, India had devised its own methods and best practices of being a non-denominational state and polity. These practices were not derived from a

Western paradigm that emphasized the neat and complete separation between state and religion. Rather, the attempt was to work towards strengthening the principles of social justice, pluralism, tolerance, and freedom of religion. Seventy-five years later, it is worth revisiting some of the founding moments of Indian secularism to see how they have fared over the decades.

In a classical liberal sense, secularism is defined by the following characteristics: a separation of Church (or any other ecclesiastical institution) and State; privatization of religion and its withdrawal from the public sphere; and protection of religious liberties. Indian secularism does not adhere to these principles as understood in their classical liberal ways. Constitutionally speaking, the Indian state does not entertain a 'wall of separation' between itself and religion but maintains a position of neutrality and even-handedness towards all religions. Providing safeguards to religious expression, freedom of religion and conscience, and minority rights are some of the key characteristics of what has been called 'Indian secularism' (Bhargava 2002). At the same time, the state also undertakes the project of social reform quite seriously, especially within its majority religion, i.e., Hinduism.

When we shift our gaze from state to society, we see that the Indian public sphere is hardly free of religion. Religion has not been privatized in the Indian context the way in which it has been done in the context of European democracies. Hence, a key characteristic of secularism, i.e., the withdrawal of religion from the public sphere into the private or personal space, is not applicable in the context of India. The situation is further compounded by the critical role that religious collectives and organizations play in the Indian context, both as sources of normative structures that govern people's lives and as sites where the 'social', broadly speaking, takes place—in extraordinary times as well as everyday life. Should these factors, then, be grounds for considering the Indian commitment to secularism as half-hearted and haphazard?

There exist a range of opinions on the precise nature of Indian secularism, whether it can be considered secularism at all, and whether it is appropriate for Indian realities. The scholarship on this topic is vast—not surprisingly, given how immediate and pertinent this issue has been since Independence and, especially, in the last few decades. Several political scientists, most prominently Rajeev Bhargava, point out that Indian constitution-makers and the state should be lauded for imagining a different kind of secular polity than the paradigmatic liberal one where state and religion are cleanly separated (i.e. the Church has no influence on the State) and the privatization of religion is fairly complete. Indian secularism, it is argued, is worthy of being considered an alternative framework of a secular polity where its key characteristics in a Western, liberal sense are modified, albeit not compromised, in ways that befit a multicultural and multi-religious society such as India's. Hence, the separation principle is modified to 'principled distance' between Church and State while the privatization principle has been modified to 'balancing the claims of individuals and religious communities' (Bhargava 2002: 2). Others have contended that secularism is a flawed concept, rooted in the specific histories of the emergence of the nation state in Western Europe, and ill-fitted to Indian realities. Moreover, it is also an alien concept, rooted in the intellectual history of Protestant Christianity and the political history of Europe, that the average Indian is unable to understand or unwilling to accept (Nandy 1995).

During the Constituent Assembly debates, several of these issues were raised and debated, often in great detail and over several days and weeks. There were proponents of a strict form of secularism, one that proposed a complete removal of religion from public life and polity, such as K. T. Shah. There were also those who were keen to maintain an overall Hindu religious framework in public ethical and moral life, such as K. M. Munshi. Often, the two sides also fell at opposite ends of the spectrum on other social issues, such as reservations for disadvantaged groups and the role of culture in society. It is worth noting that despite India's first prime minister Jawaharlal Nehru's overall understanding of religion as a force of counter-modernity, the Constitution attempted to find a middle ground between these two extreme views. It did so by delinking the state from any religious affiliation whatsoever, protecting freedom of expression (including religious expression), and adhering to principles of social reform within Hinduism, particularly with regard to caste, while ensuring political safeguards for minorities (Tejani 2007).

The key articles of the Indian Constitution that enshrine and safeguard principles of secularism are Articles 25–30. These deal with matters of freedom of religion and minority rights, and have collectively been called 'articles of faith' (Sen 2019). Article 25 and 26 deal with the right to freedom of conscience, to 'profess, practice, and propagate' religion, and to manage one's own religious institutions. Article 27 prohibits the state from using taxpayers' money to promote or fund any religion. Article 28 allows religious institutions to impart religious instruction. Article 29 deals with the protection of interests of minorities (religious as well as cultural and linguistic). And Article 30 grants the right to religious and linguistic minorities to establish and administer their own educational institutions. It is worth noting that at the beginning of the Constituent Assembly debates, 'minorities' encapsulated religious, caste, and linguistically marginalized communities. However, by the time the Constitution was adopted, the claims of religious and caste minorities 'were deemed qualitatively different', with the former being provided political safeguards and the latter becoming the recipients of affirmative action measures (Tejani 2007).

The field of law and religion in India, perhaps out of necessity given contemporary issues, has often been reduced to the question of secularism. Given that the modern state in India has to play a key role in the management of religious difference, and much of this management is done through the making and implementation of good and fair laws, this is not entirely surprising. But law and religion cannot be historically reduced to the question of secularism. The field must be studied in its totality. When we look at an issue synchronically, in all its contemporary nuances and layers, we miss out on a more historically rooted and diachronic approach. The relationship between law and religion in India is historically constituted and evolving.

Law and Religion in Pre-Colonial India

For most readers, the intersection of law and religion in contemporary India may lie at the point where law, understood as the judicial system of India as upheld by the courts, intersects with the religious practices of the people. Rarely do we pay attention to the larger framing of state and sovereignty within the ethical and moral codes that derive in no uncertain measure from religion. The Sanskrit term *dharma* is both the source and praxis of law in the Hindu sense. This concept informed state, sovereignty, and juridical authority in early India. *Dharma* in the sense of law and sovereignty (and not as duty or religion or religious practice) derives from Hindu law books composed during a vast period spanning the early centuries of the Common Era all the way up to the early centuries of the second millennium. Hindu law books were a key scriptural source of secular as well as religious law in India. The extent and precision of implementation of these Hindu texts in premodern state and juridical systems is a moot point, and for the most part the rules laid down there constituted an idealized notion of law, sovereignty, and justice.

With the coming of Muslim political rule in India, there is a discernable layering of judicial systems. By the eleventh century, Islamic law and jurisprudence had emerged as a well-developed system. Legal authorities (*muftis* and *qazis*), scriptural sources of law (Quran, Sunna, Hadith), legal institutions (*fatwas*), legal processes and reasoning (*fiqhs*) were well established, and, in principle, applicable to all the realms that fell under the Caliphate. However, much like the normative injunctions of Hindu law books, the applicability of Islamic law was limited, and the responses were contextualized within local conditions (Chatterjee 2020). In his travels, Ibn Battuta, the fourteenth-century Moroccan traveller who spent a considerable time in Sultanate India, notes several inconsistencies of legal jurisprudence and everyday practices in the region that were at variance from established law; but he seems to not be bothered by them too much.

Nonetheless, the imprecise but normatively influential jurisprudential framework of Islamic legal authorities was established at this time, with legal experts (*muftis*) and court judges (*qazis*), alongside theologians (*ulemas*) emerging as key figures of political and religious authority over the twelfth to eighteenth centuries. Rather than thinking of this as a time when the sharia was uniformly implemented on the people of South Asia, as is commonly done, scholars argue that this was a period of 'legal pluralism' of the 'Islamicate law' where a set of several overlapping customs, practices, taxation regimes, theological frameworks, local and imperial politics jostled with each other in maintaining law and order in a region (Chatterjee 2020: 3–5). The legal authorities of the time could be the Muslim judge or the legal expert alongside several other authorities, such as caste elders, scribes who noted the judgements, regional and local political elites, and religious and priestly authorities, each of whom could serve as an appellate authority against the decisions of the other, while the emperor remained the final source of all juridical authority.

This kind of unevenness around law and religion is important for us to understand, both during the so-called 'Hindu period' of Indian history as well as later. While religion remained a key source of the values and virtues of what we may call law in these times, it was hardly the only one. Also important to note is the 'lumpy landscape' of law in pre-colonial India where several kinds of customary practices jostled for space within the same region (Chatterjee 2020: 5). These customary practices could be specific

to certain religious communities, castes and sub-
castes, religious sects, and even subgroups within
castes or religious communities.

Women, Law, and Religion
in Colonial India

As the East India Company's rule expanded over
the territory of South Asia, and with the transfer
of power to the British Crown in 1858, governing
and disciplining religious practices became a bone
of contention between Indian elites and the colonial
administrators and lawmakers. Over the course of the
long nineteenth century and after, the colonial state,
in its efforts to impose a 'rule of law' to replace the
erstwhile 'despotic' forms of rule, intervened through
law in religious matters several times and in ways that
had long-term consequences. The Company, and
after 1858 the Crown, put down several legislative
measures that amounted to 'interference' in religious
matters of the 'natives'—a matter that was not appre-
ciated at all. The ban on the practice of widow immo-
lation with the deceased husband, laws outlawing
hook-swinging, stricter public health-related administration of prominent religious pilgrimage sites such
as Puri or Haridwar during festival season, raising the

minimum age of marriage and consummation for girls, regulating divorce and maintenance of widows, and translating religious and pilgrimage sites into the concepts of 'trusts' and 'property' which were subject to certain kinds of regulatory and fiscal regimes, were some of the key transformations brought about by the colonial state as a consequence of its avowed adherence to the 'rule of law' and 'rule of property'. Not surprisingly, despite the professed secularism of the colonial administration, Indian elites not only experienced it as a form of religious interference and, at times, persecution, they also mounted an opposition to colonial rule in religious and cultural terms.

The English East India Company, for the very first time, attempted to uniformly apply Hindu and Muslim law on populations that identified themselves as one or the other. This was not an easy task. Introducing a Western-derived uniformity over the uneven landscape of Indian legal mores and customs was far from smooth. Company officials had to deal with an unfamiliar legal system, with vast differences in the application of criminal and civil—as well as fiscal—regimes across regions and communities. In searching for uniformity, the colonial state, driven by orientalist principles, ascertained scripture to be the source of what all Hindus and Muslims recognized as law. Officials of the colonial state sat with a handful of experts on scripture in order to put together a 'code of laws' that could be applied by the colonial courts in adjudicating cases. This was called Anglo-Indian Law in the late eighteenth century, and it was most often used to decide matters of property dispute for taxation purposes. The right to *diwani* (revenue collection) gained by the East India Company for the province of Bengal in 1765 meant that the Company needed to find ways to address property disputes in the region, assess taxation schedules, and determine landownership. Customary law was found to be extremely varied across groups and communities, and unsuited for the uniform fiscal management the Company desired. Hence, Company officials turned to the pandits in Calcutta and Banaras to find a common source for Hindu law. In the late eighteenth century for the very first time, Manu's *Dharmashastra* was deemed to be the central law book governing the practices of all Hindus living in Company-ruled territories in India.

With the strengthening of the system of colonial courts and litigation, and the consequent creation of the colonized people as legal subjects, the colonial officials found themselves sitting on cases that dealt not merely with property disputes but also with other kinds of family disputes around issues of succession and inheritance, maintenance, adoption, and divorce. The British, during the nineteenth century, devised a form of legal pluralism in India whereby personal and family law was separated from public and criminal law (Lhost 2022). Hence, Hindus and Muslims in colonial India received separate legal systems that governed their private lives. At the same time, these personal laws were made more uniform and homogenous for different religious communities. There was a flattening-out of the 'lumpy landscape' of jurisprudence from pre-colonial times when custom, community, and state authorities, rather than an abstract notion of law, reigned supreme. In the process, the practices of community elites that, more often than not, tended towards being conservative, were strengthened and uniformly applied to all members of that religious group. This placed subjects, particularly women, solely and entirely within the purview of orthodox scriptural codes interpreted by men. This had far-reaching ramifications for the range of people who were now to be governed by this law in matters relating to family affairs, particularly marriage, divorce, and inheritance. It also laid the foundations for something that would take shape decades later—i.e. religious identities as recognizable legal and juridical categories that could avail themselves of special commissions granted to them under law.

One of the abiding tensions of the practice of modern law and jurisprudence in India has been the question of the family—particularly women and all matters concerning them. In the colonial period, women became the key site of conflict between Indian elites and the colonial state, and it was seen as a nationalist imperative to keep women and matters relating to them outside interference by the 'foreign' state and its lawmakers. A noteworthy outcome of this effort to keep matters relating to women out of colonial courts and within the purview of community elders was the gradual reticence shown by the colonial government to legislate on family matters. Even as sati had been banned in 1829, similar steps to push for more egalitarian laws for women received tremendous pushback from the communities involved, as seen in the public outcry against the Age of Consent Bill of the late nineteenth century. By the mid-nineteenth century, each religious community in India—Hindus, Muslims, Parsis, and Christians—had their own family law or Personal Law. This meant that each identifiably religious community was differently governed in matters of marriage, divorce, maintenance, inheritance, and so on (Nair 1996).

While these codified Personal Laws brought Muslim and Hindu women much more strongly within the ambit of their respective communities and its scriptural sanctions, they also derecognized regional and caste-based variations (Nair 1996). The family laws for Hindus were implemented by the British courts, and hence were liable to face further reform on liberal lines. For Muslims, Personal Laws were implemented by recognized religio-legal authorities of the community who would be trained in one or other Islamic seminary in India, the most prominent of which was at Deoband. The Sikhs, Jains, and Buddhists were governed by Hindu Personal Laws implemented by the courts.

The debates around the Uniform Civil Code in contemporary India, thus, go back to the late nineteenth century, with the introduction of Personal Laws. Post-Independence, while the legislature assumed responsibility to reform Hindu Personal Laws, often in accordance with a recognizably liberal and rights-based framework of gender relations, these laws were systematically left within the purview of community elders and religious authorities as part of constitutionally guaranteed protection to religious minorities. Reform within Hindu Personal Laws was not an easy process. There was considerable opposition to granting equal rights of property, divorce, and maintenance to women. It is noteworthy that the Hindu Code Bill took several years to pass in the Parliament of Independent India and did so in 1956 only after being broken up into four separate Acts. Contemporary debates over the Uniform Civil Code in India need to take this uneven history into account and, as legal and constitutional expert Gautam Bhatia has argued, be rearticulated through a language of gender justice rather than the current communally polarized language that they have become mired in (Bhatia 2022).

Religion, the Courts, and Law in Independent India

In the Indian context, the courts have been called upon to adjudicate on several matters pertaining to religion since the introduction of the colonial judicial system. Since Independence, the Indian courts have adjudicated cases that range from determining what is essentially religious and what lies outside it, to the management of religious difference, the protection of minority rights, ensuring religious reform, and regulating the relationship between religion and the state. Key court cases from the colonial and postcolonial period allow us to see how case law sets a precedent that impinges upon the relationship between law and religion in contemporary India. Focusing on two such concepts—first, the juridical personhood of Hindu deities and, second, the Essential Religious Practices test—will help clarify how law and religion intersect in contemporary India.

A juristic personality is a legal construct, just like the legal personality of humans. The notion of juristic personality originates in Roman Law, and is applied to trusts, organizations, and corporations in modern law. During the nineteenth century, when governing authorities of religious sites came into conflict with colonial law, often on grounds of paying taxes or ownership of property, the Hindu deity was recognized as a juristic personality under law on a par with trusts and corporations. However, the deity was a juristic person only insofar as it remained a minor and was represented by a person, often the chief priest of the idol and the sacred space (the temple and its grounds) 'owned' by the idol. This particular feature of colonial law allowed the peculiar vital or 'alive' and personal nature of Hindu deities to be lawfully recognized and admitted into legal proceedings. In order to do so, colonial courts established that any Hindu idol that was under continuous and unbroken worship by a priest or intermediary could be considered a juristic personality if it was represented by the same caretaker or priest (Bagchi 1933).

This very legal aspect played a key role in the manner in which the Ram Janmabhumi court case was adjudicated by the Supreme Court in 2019. Various components from the Sangh Parivar—the broad conglomeration of political, cultural, social, and educational organizations committed to the cause of Hindutva—played an active role in this dispute. The case related to a 150-year-old property dispute, initially between a Ramanandi *akhara* and the Waqf Board over the site where the Babri Masjid once stood. In the late nineteenth century, colonial courts refrained from handing over the disputed site to either party. As a result, local Muslims continued to offer prayers while several Hindus continued to conduct worship within the larger compound of the mosque at a spot that was claimed by many interested parties as the birthplace of the Hindu deity Rama. In 1949, an idol of Rama as a child miraculously 'appeared' on that spot, thereby opening up the possibility of considering this image as the ruling deity and a juristic personality—capable of representing itself in a court of law. Later investigations showed that this idol had been placed inside the erstwhile mosque with the help of the district collector of Ayodhya, a person sympathetic to the Hindu organization Rashtriya Swayamsevak Sangh (RSS). The dispute emerged as a game-changer in Indian politics and social relations. The currently ruling Bharatiya Janata Party took up the cause of building a temple to Rama on this spot, now widely held to be his birthplace, as its key objective. In December 1992, *kar sevaks* (volunteers) from RSS and its affiliate organizations dismantled the structure of the Babri Masjid, leading to serious interreligious strife and rioting across the country.

While these historical, political, and social aspects of the Babri Masjid–Ram Janmabhumi dispute are well known, what is less known is its importance as a legal case that draws upon juridical developments from the past 150 years (Kapur 2023). In 2019, the Supreme Court decided to hand over the entire contested land to Ram Lalla, the infant Rama, represented by the Ram Janmabhumi Trust. The 2019 judgement took into account the beliefs of the Hindus that the contested site was the birthplace of Rama together with the juristic personhood of Hindu deities in making its judgement. Interestingly, apart from nullifying the claims of the Sunni Waqf Board, this move fundamentally delegitimized the claims of contending Hindu monastic institutions to a share in the part of the property that now belonged exclusively to Ram Lalla, the Ram Janmabhumi, and his sole representative, the Ram Janmabhumi Trust. The judgement shifted the legal foundations of the case from a property dispute to a claim around freedom of religion, thereby making it about the faith of the

Hindu community and their freedom of expression (Kapur 2023).

The Ram Janmabhumi–Babri Masjid dispute has been a defining one for India in the last few decades. However, this is by no means the first time that the courts in India have played a decisive role in religious matters; and it will not be the last. In fact, by the 1950s, a large body of case law had developed in India with regard to Hindu religious endowments (Derrett 1963; Fuller 1988). Since Independence, the courts have been actively adjudicating on matters relating to religion in India, not only property disputes but also the scope, extent, and nature of religious practices. In the past seventy-five years, Indian courts have been asked to adjudicate upon matters as complex and varied as the entry of women into sacred spaces, the ritual of fasting unto death, and whether a person who does not hail from a particular sub-clan of Brahmins can be made a priest in a particular temple. Taken together, these cases make up the considerable case law that reflects the close relationship between law and religion in post-Independence India. And one of the key formulations that such deliberations have led to is the Essential Religious Practices test, which allows the courts and judges to decide whether or not a particular practice falls within the purview of an 'essential' practice, without which the very foundations of a person's religious beliefs will fail. If determined to be the former, the courts will let the matter remain as it is, and not interfere in it. If decided to be the latter, the courts allow for interference and change in those practices.

In a 1954 decision by the Supreme Court, in what is known as the Shirur Mutt case (*Commissioner of Hindu Religious Endowments, Madras* v. *Shri Lakshmindra Thirtha Swamiar, Shirur*), the kernel of what later came to be called the Essential Religious Practices test was laid down. In the words of the honourable court, 'what constitutes the essential part of a religion is primarily to be ascertained with reference to the doctrines of that religion itself' (quoted in Fuller 1988: 228). In 1961, in the Durgah Committee judgement (*Durgah Committee, Ajmer* v. *Syed Hussain Ali*), this definition was tightened to remove 'superstitious practices' and secular concerns masquerading as religious ones from the purview of essential religious practices. However, this has ensured that the courts in India have the power to decide on the essential aspects of a religion—a decision that they frequently take based upon textual evidence found in the scriptures of a particular religion (Fuller 1988). In the past, the courts have decided to uphold the right of a particular religious institution to employ priests from a particular caste, based upon the *Agamas* and other ritual texts that determined the rituals and practices of that temple (Fuller 1988). In another key decision, in what is known as the Satsang Case of 1966 (*Shastri Yagnapurashdasji* v. *Muldas Bhundardas Vaishya*), the court rejected a plea made by members of the Swaminarayana sect to not follow the provisions of the temple entry legislation of 1947. The plea was made on the grounds that they were distinct and different from Hindu religion and hence the said legislation did not apply to them. Upon scrutinizing the tenets and practices of the sect, the court ruled that it was, indeed, a Hindu sect in its essential religious practices (Fuller 1988).

More recently, the Essential Religious Practices test has been applied to court cases dealing with the Jain practice of *sallekhana* or *santhara*, whereby a Jain practitioner takes a vow to gradually reduce and eventually cease partaking of food and water until their death. This practice was challenged in the courts by petitioners who claimed that the traditional vow ought to be considered a form of suicide and hence was in contravention of the right to life enshrined in Article 21. While the Rajasthan High Court made the practice unlawful in 2015 (*Nikhil Soni* v. *Union of India and Ors.*), the Supreme Court stayed the order in less than a month. In a different vein, the Karnataka High Court ruled in a 2022 judgement (*Smt Resham*

v. *State of Karnataka*) that the practice of wearing a headscarf over school uniform in government schools was not an essential religious practice, since the meaning of hijab itself had been debated within Islamic jurisprudence and there was no consensus over what it entailed. Scholars of law and religion argue that the Essential Religious Practices test shifts the focus from practice to scriptural aspects of religion, thereby further dismissing popular religious practices that fall outside scriptural sanction (Kapur 2023). This shift is in itself a result of colonial modes of regulating and governing religious communities (Sen 2019).

Conclusion

It is important to recognize that far from being a distant and objective observer, law plays a very significant role in determining the religious life worlds of Indians today. As Manisha Sethi writes, '[i]f religion is not an ahistorical abstraction comprehensible only through symbols but created and forged in the furnace of power, law can be seen playing a key role in tempering it. It is one of the key discourses through which religion is constituted' (Sethi 2019: 110). As we have seen, law determines what are the essential religious practices of a tradition, regulates fiscal and other explicitly secular aspects of religious trusts and the spaces they administer, and exercises control over everyday piety and religious articulations, from the clothes people wear to the spaces they can or cannot access. At times, law bears the mantle of liberal reform; at other times, it upholds tradition. In all regards, the courts in India have paid careful attention to religious scriptures and practices, as well as to the necessity of reform. Arguably, such legal interference cements what exists through constitutional measures already—that the Indian state has devised a form of secular polity that is vastly different from Western frameworks of secularism.

5

Media and Religious Publics

Since the Protestant Reformation in Europe in the sixteenth century, rational faith has been considered to be one that is based on interiority, individual piety, and a direct access to God through prayer and leading a moral life. This has led to one of the most common misconceptions about religion—that it is an unmediated phenomenon. Nothing could be further from the truth. Religion is a mediated and, in the current digitally driven media ecology, highly mediatized phenomenon. Religious actors and authorities have historically made use of all kinds of media—from the body to materials such as stone and metal, to language and sound—in order to communicate and transmit religious experiences, practices, and doctrines. The modern period has witnessed a sharp increase in the use of media technologies in the service of religion.

Religion in India. Varuni Bhatia, Oxford University Press.
© Varuni Bhatia 2025. DOI: 10.1093/oso/9780198958345.003.0006

Irrespective of which faith we speak of, religious individuals, groups, and organizations in the modern period have been extremely savvy regarding their use of media. To a large extent, how we understand, practise, and preach religion is largely determined by the media moment we inhabit and by the media technologies available to us, so much so that the notion of divinity variously reveals itself in multiple ways—through narrative, discourse, and practice—by the use of technology. This invites us to understand religion and technology, especially media technology, not as lying at opposite ends of the analytical spectrum but as deeply constitutive of each other (Stolow 2013).

The intersection between media and religion becomes even more significant when we shift our focus from individuals and organizations to religious collectives. A unified collective of otherwise spatially and temporally dispersed people is only possible with the use of means of communication. Thus, for example, the nation depended heavily upon the use of print technology to emerge as the most prominent collective in the modern period. The idea that a shared history, culture, language, and religion could bind together communities spread over large geographical areas was only possible with the coming of print and its extensive usage as a medium of nationalist propagation. Apart from the nation, religion became the other key modern collective to emerge from the use of media technologies. The notion that one was a Hindu or a Muslim or a Christian like any other Hindu or Christian or Muslim in the rest of the world, irrespective of one's local contexts, was significantly abetted by the rise and spread of print.

Since the appearance of print, and especially in the twentieth century, media technologies have witnessed a rapid evolution. Developments in sound and audiovisual media technologies, the coming of analog media transmission, and the recent developments in digital technology have had a transformative impact on the constitution of religious collectives and publics. Today, it is no longer surprising to find large religious collectives variously expressing themselves over different kinds of media platforms—from older forms of print and analog media to more recent digital media. Practically every type and form of religious expression—from everyday religious practices to religious festivals, religious discourses by experts, instructions on how to conduct oneself appropriately in religious matters, scriptural study courses, lifestyle advice for the faithful, and so on—is easily available in print and audiovisual media, including on our screens and digital devices. Simultaneously, the role of media in generating religious affect, sometimes of a negative kind, has also been widely observed by scholars as well as social commentators. The intersection of religion and media thus allows us to look at these several dimensions of our religious present—from the increasingly mediatized practice of religion to the formation of religious publics and their affective engagement with civic life.

Print and Nationalist Public in Colonial India

The consolidation of religious publics, their mobilization and repurposing for non-religious or political ends, is not new in the subcontinent's modern history. It is a process that stretches at least as far back as the coming of print technology to the subcontinent. The origin of print is itself closely intertwined with religion. The first book ever to be printed globally was the Bible. In India, too, the earliest printed literature in regional Indian languages was closely associated with missionary activities in various languages, predominantly Tamil, Konkani, and Bengali (Frykenberg 2008). The Jesuits, followed by the Baptists, were at the forefront of developing and standardizing scripts, producing grammars and dictionaries in several Indian languages in order to facilitate the printing of Christian texts, the Bible, the Gospels, prayer books, and catechisms in those languages. The moveable type that thus emerged evolved into the standard script for several, if not most, Indian languages. By the nineteenth century, missionary-run presses, such as the Baptist Press at Serampore in Bengal, were also at the forefront of printing and publishing Hindu mythologies and scriptures. The aim was to learn about Indian religions, primarily Hinduism, in order to refute it. Hence, from the very beginning of the nineteenth century, print technology played a formative role in preparing the ground for religious discussion and debate in modern India.

The printed word was suffused with religious didacticism in the period of high nationalism in India. Religious texts were already being published, first by missionaries and missionary-run presses, and then by fledgling publishing enterprises set up by Indians themselves that would eventually grow into large publishing houses. Several printing presses that were set up in the nineteenth and twentieth centuries specialized in religious and didactic literature along-side topics of social reform, gender relations, education, nationalism, entertainment, and even politics. There are several examples of well-known printing presses that were deeply involved in publishing religious literature: Gita Press in Gorakhpur, Bangabasi Press in Calcutta, Venkateshwara Press in Bombay, and Naval Kishore Press in Lucknow are some of the names more prominently associated with religious literature. These presses published religious myths and legends, instruction manuals, commentaries, translations, didactic literature, and images. Across religious divides, faith-based journals, instruction manuals, and periodicals played the role of the religious authority, the theologian, and the priest throughout the latter half of the nineteenth century and well into the twentieth. The Gita Press, established in 1923, for instance, was a huge factor in the popularity of Hindu religious and didactic literature. It publishes one of the most successful printed books in India—the *Bhagavad Gita* in the original with a Hindi translation (Mukul 2015). Similarly, the number of printed versions of Muslim pietistic and didactic texts soared in the twentieth century with texts such as Maulana Ashraf 'Ali Thanvi's *Bihishti Zewar* rapidly reaching middle-class Muslim households, especially women, across north India (Metcalf 1992). The role of the religious expert and specialist played by print culture did not diminish in the following decades until the emergence of the digital medium.

The emergence of popular printing in India, from the mid-nineteenth century onwards, was largely driven by a demand for cheap publications. Simultaneously, woodcut printing technology made it possible, for the first time, to bring alive, on the pages of a printed book, images of Hindu gods and goddesses. This ironic juxtaposition drove up the demand for cheap and inexpensive versions of both kinds of texts: religious manuals and posters of gods and sacred places vied with each other in inexpensive markets of published materials such as *Battala* in colonial Calcutta. Religious posters, in particular, received a fillip through the vast demand for them (Pinney 2004). Earlier, a deity or a theological concept could only be represented in iconic or aniconic forms using organic or natural materials such as wood or stone or clay or painted manuscript—all of which were labour-intensive to produce and required considerable resources to maintain them. However, with the dawn of cheaply available posters of gods, it became increasingly more convenient and inexpensive both to place a representation of a deity in one's home or workplace, however humble, and to insert these images into printed religious texts, thereby adding another layer of sacrality to the otherwise profane world of print. The printing presses in various parts of India produced their own characteristic kinds of posters of gods (Davis 2012). It is worth noting that this 'mechanical reproduction' of a sacred object did render it less sacred at times—and it was not unusual to find images of gods and sacred spaces on commercial objects such as matchboxes, tea packets, or textiles (Jain 2007).

These sacred posters, due to their widespread dissemination, were critical in producing a devotional sensibility as well as religious community. The manner in which Raja Ravi Varma painted Hindu deities, for instance, left a long-lasting impact on how they have been imagined up to the present day, down to the colour of the skin, the contours of the body, and the placement of various gods and goddesses in relation to each other. The iconicity of Bharat Mata images is also traceable to this period. At the turn of the twentieth century, and well into the 1940s, Bharat Mata posters of several kinds were being printed and sold in an unprecedented fashion. A large number of posters showed Bharat Mata—imagined specifically as a Puranic, Hindu deity—in a geospatial imagination where the contours of India appeared as the embodied form of the goddess (Ramaswamy 2010). The geospatial imagination drew heavily on the Hindu theological understanding of sacred space as an embodiment of the deity residing within it. Without needing any special explication, Bharat Mata posters effectively and pointedly conveyed to anti-colonial and nationalist Indians the message of India as a sacred land personified as a goddess who demanded devotion through acts of patriotism.

Print—both the printed word and the printed image—contributed in a substantial fashion to the rising communalism in pre-Independence India which led to unsurmountable cleavages between Hindus and Muslims. Large campaigns that brought Hindus together across castes and regions, such as the Shuddhi (purifying), Sangathan (community building and organizing), and cow-protection campaigns from the 1920s onwards, depended heavily on the print medium to propagate their message. These were further amplified, quite literally, by the association of loudspeaker technologies that changed how devotional music and religious sermons were disseminated. Thus, in the decades that led up to the partition of British India, media technologies of various types had proven to be an effective handmaiden in how religious identities were fixed and religious communities were forged as political actors.

Cinema and the Devotional Public in Post-Independence India

Dadasaheb Phalke, the first Indian to make a film, had famously embarked upon his film-making career because he wanted to see Indian images on-screen—more precisely, images of Hindu gods and goddesses.

Phalke may have been amongst the earliest pioneers to recognize the immense potential that lay in the ocular medium of cinema which could effectively translate into a coherent narrative the affect, charisma, and awe of Hindu forms of devotion and religiosity. Over the next hundred years, cinema would deeply engage with and influence religion in India, on registers far beyond the imagination of its early proponent. Cinema draws together citizenship, community, and modernity in the context of religion in ways that no other media has been able to do in the Indian context. As Rachel Dwyer notes, 'Indian cinema more than any other media, whether newspapers or the novel ... has mediated the imagination of the Indian nation' (Dwyer 2006: 1). Dwyer notes that this is because of the sheer depth of reach of cinema in India, as well as the consumption of cinema beyond its on-screen presence—through music, radio, television, magazines, etc. In many ways, the same can be said of how cinema and its extra-cinematic excess, particularly through music and techno-devotion, has 'mediated the imagination' of religion in twentieth-century India.

By the mid-twentieth century, literacy rates in India were still quite low. While the religious and devotional print culture had had a tremendous impact on how the literate and semi-literate sections of Indian society engaged with their religious practices, direct access to printed material—especially material that needed to be read—was still limited. In this regard, cinema emerged in the early twentieth century as a new mode of engagement with the divine—a technologically produced and mediated engagement that was able to bring together the ocular and wondrous dimensions of religious experience alongside its narrative elements. Drawing upon the rich tradition of popular and folk theatre from various parts of India, cinema for the very first time in India physically brought together a large affective public whose interaction with the big screen would not cease after it had left the cinema theatres.

Film critics and scholars of Indian cinema have located the emergence of a cultural modernism in the rise of cinematic publics in India. The golden age of cinema in India is identified in the decades immediately following Independence, when cinema represented a modern polity and state. It articulated, on the one hand, a clear critique of old, feudal forms, while offering, on the other, a secular and socialist utopia of a new India. At the same time, historians of film as well as scholars of popular culture have been quick to point out that cinema in India has never entirely rid itself of religion (Dwyer 2006; Bhrugubanda 2018). Some of the earliest films in any Indian language dealt with religious subjects, such as *Sant Tukaram* in Marathi and *Raja Harishchandra* in Hindi—a trend that continued well into the later decades of the twentieth century, even after the emergence of national cinema in the decades after Independence, dealing with themes such as socialism and national unity. Religious and devotional themes in cinema continued to provide blockbuster hits—as evidenced by the unexpected and runaway success of *Jai Santoshi Ma* released in 1975 in Hindi.

New intersections between cinema, politics, and language-based identities appeared in post-Independence India. The growth of the southern film industry, and the film stars who turned into extremely popular and powerful public figures floating their own political parties, brought into focus the role played by charisma and devotionally charged fan collectives around these figures. Analysing the success of film-star-turned-successful-politicians N. T. Rama Rao and M. G. Ramachandran, film scholar Madhav Prasad notes that their films represent 'cine-politics' whereby cinema becomes the instrument of political messaging and political mobilization (Prasad 2009). Taking the observation further, S. V. Srinivas notes in his study of Telugu stardom the overlap between a new kind of fan public and the charisma of a film star from which it arose—a fandom that lends itself to comparison with the act of devotion or *bhakti* itself. This new film and film-star bhakti public is then seamlessly available for political mobilization outside cinema spaces (Srinivas 2013). In her recent work on Telugu mythological films, Uma Bhrugubanda also notes the sheer appeal of religious-themed cinema to audiences, in a manner that creates the larger-than-life, almost godlike film star as well as the devotional publics that affectively respond to that star (Bhrugubanda 2018).

Cinema has been an extremely powerful medium in India. It has played both a contentious and a complicit role in the making of the Indian nation and its majoritarian culture, its regional linguistic articulations, and its affective, often melodramatic, publics. It has not only been a particularly fitting medium for the transmission of the wondrous elements of religion in an audiovisual form, but has also helped forge religious practices for contemporary Indian publics. The social and practised aspect of religion as portrayed in cinema has impacted the pietistic and devotional practices of Indians. For example, *Jai Santoshi Ma* was a landmark film that led to the immense popularity of this lesser-known goddess, especially amongst women viewers and devotees. It also remains one of the few blockbuster Hindi films dealing with the widespread Hindu women's pietistic practices around the *vrat katha* (vows and rituals based on legends). Depiction of religion in cinema covers themes as varied as the salubrious effects of pilgrimage, the powers of a guru or a deity or a sacred space, and the impact of true faith and belief in the divine. Some films have also been unabashed in critiquing superstitious religious practices, although these have been fewer in number. More recently, for example in *Adipurush* (2023), the issue of taking offence over the depiction of deities on-screen has also been observed.

However, cinematic excess—the residue of cinema outside cinema halls—is where some of the more long-lasting aspects of the engagement between religion and cinema can be located. Audio tapes of devotional music based upon the tunes of film songs are par for the course in contemporary India, across religious boundaries. Audio technology, in fact, has been a critical medium of religious content, with such content from across various traditions finding its way into peoples' homes and public religious sites. It is impossible in this context not to recall the immense popularity of devotional songs sung by Anuradha Paudwal and released on inexpensive T-Series tapes. The techno-devotional special effects of cinema, particularly the striking visuals and special effects that accompany the appearance of deities or miracles on-screen, are reproduced off-screen and within temple precincts, using a wide array of light and sound effects (Srinivas 2018). It is not unusual at the present time to see cameras recording all kinds of rituals and rites within Hindu temples, including the broadcasting of 'live darshan' by prominent temples such as Siddhivinayak in Mumbai and ISKCON in Bangalore. These can be viewed from the comfort of one's home, over internet-supported devices. In many ways, cinematic publics bleed into broadcast publics in contemporary India, in their consumption of religious images, discourses, and messages.

Television and the Broadcast Public

The television series *Ramayan*, produced by Ramanand Sagar, forever changed the nature of religious publics and their relationship to citizenship in India. This is attested by contemporary news reports commenting on the empty streets and bazaars every Sunday morning when the serial was telecast on national television. It is buttressed by memories of people of varying ages who recall gathering around the one television unit in a neighbourhood, worshipping the object like it was a deity, and then watching the *lila* (divine play) of Ram play itself out on the small screen. Scholars have analysed how Sagar and his team deftly deployed the technology and skills of film-making to produce special effects that, on the one hand, highlighted the darshan dimensions of storytelling and, on the other, handed the experience of being a devotee, a *bhakta*, to the multitudinous and enraptured audience (Rajagopal 2001). As Philip Lutgendorf remarked, noting the peculiar confluence of broadcast media and devotionally themed content, 'Never before had such a large percentage of South Asia's population been united in a single activity; never before had a single message instantaneously reached so enormous a regional audience' (Lutgendorf 1990: 128). The television *Ramayan* was a landmark moment in India when we think about the relationship between media and religion. In its ability to bring together film tech-nology, the broadcast medium of state-owned televi-sion, and a remarkably unified devotional collective that grew around its weekly screening, the *Ramayan* was a tour de force. However, the attention that this event has received ought not to make us forget other forms of broadcast media that have been used over the twentieth century.

There are key broadcast media that have remained under-examined in the Indian context, especially in their contribution to forging religious publics of dif-ferent kinds. These are the radio, the audio cassette, and the VHS tape. All India Radio systematically organized its programming to be secular but, at the same time, it often broadcast devotional songs sung by established maestros. In Bengal each year, the strains of the *Mahalaya*—a recitation of the Sanskrit devotional song in praise of the goddess Durga—by Birendra Krishna Bhadra can be heard from the wee hours of the morning on the first day of the autumnal goddess festival of Durga Puja. The short-lived VHS tape technology also played an important role, especially in serving as didactic and publicity material. Like the loudspeaker and the audio tape, the VHS tape also amplified, albeit in an audiovisual format, key incidents that could be used to incite violence. It became a favourite medium of expressing hate speech and disseminating violence, especially during and in the wake of the Ram Janmabhumi movement and the demolition of the Babri Masjid by Hindutva mobs (Manuel 1993). Similarly, the audio cassette technology was deployed by the Sikh preacher Jarnail Singh Bhindrawale to propagate Khalistan amongst his audiences (Jeffrey 2021). The amplificatory features of the loudspeaker, the audio cassette, and the VHS tape would later become even more intensified with the coming of digital tech-nology and its use in new media. In his study of Hindutva-pop stars in north India, Kunal Purohit shows how live performances, audio cassettes,

YouTube shorts and videos, as well as candid videos produced on smartphone cameras, serve to make the often hateful content of these local music stars go viral (Purohit 2023).

Digital Technology and the Viral Public

On 21 September 1995, news of Ganesha drinking milk spread like wildfire across the nation. Today, we would certainly call it an early incidence of a religious event 'going viral'. After the initial 'event' in Delhi in the wee hours of the morning, Ganesha statues were soon drinking milk, served to them on a spoon, all over the world. Reports from the time and even later suggest that the telephone, especially the newly introduced international calling service, played a very big role in the spread of this information—amongst both Indian middle-class Hindus and diasporic Hindus. A more recent analysis of the incident attributes the 'miracle' to careful planning and execution by the Vishwa Hindu Parishad. Once a Ganesha statue at Jhandewala in Delhi, near the Rashtriya Swayamsevak Sangh (RSS) headquarters, had 'drunk milk' at 3 a.m., telephone calls were frantically made to American Hindus who confirmed that their Ganesha idols were also drinking milk. In the morning, those out on their early walks or buying daily provisions for their homes heard the news of the so-called miracle, and disseminated it further by calling up their friends and relatives in other neighbourhoods, cities, and towns. Soon, Ganesha statues all over India and the world were reportedly drinking milk (Raman 2020).

The Ganesha milk-drinking incident is valuable in examining the intersection between media and religion in India. While it was almost certainly orchestrated by a religious organization with global networks, it failed to draw support from key political actors of the time. The scientific community also steadfastly denied its miraculous elements and, in fact, went out of its way to explain the incident through the principles of surface tension in physics. Priests of prominent Ganesha temples, particularly in Mumbai, denied that their Ganesha icons were drinking milk. Nonetheless, 21 September 1995 resulted in throngs of people queuing up outside roadside shrines, small and big temples, and even homes, to feed milk to Ganesha statues. Milk prices soared across the country. And religious organizations made statements that this was an indication of more to come. It would not be until the next day that some of the bruhaha would die down.

The medium here was the telephone. The telephone was neither an innocuous nor a serendipitous player in this story. Since the mid-1980s, due to the efforts and interest in modernizing communications, telephone technology had received a huge boost. By the late 1980s and early 1990s, telephone calls had become easier to make, telephone booths were cropping up across the country, including in small towns and rural areas, and international calling services had become available to ordinary citizens of the country. Interestingly, the telephone as a means of popular communication arrived in India through the pioneering introduction of digital technology, as opposed to the electromagnetic technology used in telephones in the West.

The use of digital technology at the intersection of religion has seen a sharp increase in the past decade or so, with the introduction of the smartphones in India. India has, quite appropriately, been termed 'cell phone nation' (Jeffrey and Doron 2013). A vast number of Indians have access to mobile phones, especially smartphones, and, in a significant divergence from Western nations, access internet via their mobile smartphones. This has led to a density of app-based sociality, economy, and even polity. The Indian government has put in place policies and infrastructures that have vastly abetted this digitalization of everyday life in India. As a result, the smartphone, a digital device, has become the instrument of accessing everything and anything—from government-led benefit schemes to popular entertainment and even news. It has also led to the explosion of the gig economy that is now a considerable dimension of the labour and workforce in India. And this has rapidly but thoroughly transformed religious engagement amongst people, both individually and collectively.

Scholars of religion and new media have been quick to point out that a pious and devoted person can easily find a plethora of things online—from religious teachings imparted by authorities to attending religious services, conducting rituals, and finding a religious community. Things are no different in India, and the realms of religious experience, didactics, and practice have increasingly become media-saturated in the specific digital format that we see today (Zeiler 2020). Several temples, gurdwaras, and churches stream their services live for their devotees. Examples include the ISKCON temple at Bangalore, the Siddhivinayak Temple at Mumbai, Harmandir Sahib (the Golden Temple) in Amritsar, Gurudwara Bangla Sahib in Delhi, and the Velankanni Shrine Basilica. Many offer special online puja and prayer services to worshippers. Gurus and religious authorities have been particularly adept at using new media technologies. From cultural aspects such as marriages to didactic aspects such as faith-based sermons, digital media has emerged as one of the most prominent sites of religious dissemination in the Indian as well as the diasporic context.

One of the key aspects of digital media content that impacts the public consuming this content is intermediality. Related to this is virality. Arguably, these two together form the centre around which the mediated and mediatized publics of contemporary India revolve. Intermediality refers to the intersections of various media forms that exist in a more recently emergent mediated space—such as print kitsch that reappears in digital images circulating over WhatsApp or cinematic special effects that accompany audiovisual content on YouTube or WhatsApp. In a highly media-saturated religious digital space, intermediality plays an important role in generating a sense of 'eternal return' of the divine presence— what Mircea Eliade noted as the essential feature of any religious ritual and sacred space (Eliade 1959). Similarly, virality helps to build community with the same content being shared, liked, and consumed by large numbers (Bhatia 2020).

Religious preachers across traditions have cultivated a successful online presence in recent years. Examples of religious figures with prominent social media presence range from the widely popular Tamil Pentecostal preacher Paul Dhinakaran, to Hindu gurus with a prominent diasporic presence, such as Sri Sri Ravishankar and Sadhguru, to the charismatic appeal of Mata Amritanandamayi. While the presence of each of these figures is seen across digital media platforms such as Twitter/X, YouTube, and OTT (Over the Top), some have been much more successful on certain media spaces than on others. Hence, one can see how Baba Ramdev of Patanjali yoga and Ayurvedic products rode to his astounding popularity through the intermedial deployment of cable television (Aastha TV), a network of yoga and Ayurvedic healing institutions (Patanjali Yogapeeth), and a very successful business venture based on commerce in Ayurvedic and herbal products and packaged goods (Patanjali Ayurved). Digital media platforms and their confluences allow for a specifically global reach for these figures. Indian preachers are able to gain huge followings in the diaspora, while non-Indian preachers, such as the Evangelist preacher Benny Hinn, are able to reach massive audiences in India (Thomas 2008).

No discussion of digital religion, especially in the context of India, can disregard the vast network of extreme speech around religion, particularly as done by the votaries of Hindutva (Udupa 2018). From outright hate speech against religious minorities to app-based incitements to violence, offensive memes, shorts, and reels stereotyping religious communities, the digital medium and its viral publics have been peculiarly well suited to disseminating content that deepens the polarizing distance between faith-based communities that exists in the country. While it would be easy to chart this up to some kind of timeless and essential difference between religious groups and faiths, for our purpose it is much more meaningful to examine how a certain kind of mediatized sociality is able to produce such a stark degree of polarization. An insight into this lies in the affordances of digitally powered social media. Anonymity, coupled with enablers to virality such as limited character messages, use of emojis, easy shareability across platforms, easy access to producing and consuming deep fakes, all abet a far more polarizing potential than has been enabled by any other media technology in the past. Such effects are being seen across all kinds of engagements, not merely the religious. While religious polarization and hateful content of a majoritarian kind have steeply increased in the wake of social media, it would be incorrect to assume that there is anything essentially religious about this rise. It is, quite simply, a product of the media worlds that we currently inhabit.

Conclusion

Media and religion are closely intertwined all over the world. While India is not singular in this regard, it offers unique insights into the workings of this relationship. The Indian case demonstrates how media technologies and media infrastructures can aid a very public nature of religion to flourish. Unlike the Western case, where the use of media technologies has been understood to contribute to the privatization of religion and the enhancement of secularism, in India media has played a central role in the continued importance of religion in the public, civic, and political life of the nation. In addition, media has been and continues to be a constitutive factor in the forging of large-scale publics in India. These publics are often, though not always, produced along religious lines and have widespread ramifications in the realm of politics as well. At the same time, for a vast majority of users and consumers of religious content on various media platforms, this simply entails a simpler, hassle-free, and, ironically, even unmediated access to their faith and faith-based practices. It is this contradiction—between private and public, religious and political, *deus ex machina* and *deus in machina*—that drives this most ephemeral and yet most significant aspect of religious life in contemporary India.

Religion and the Nation

God/s. Awe. Experience. Faith. Community. Ethics. Reason. Ritual. Discipline. There are many ways in which people understand and experience religion. And a small, but important, group defines itself against religion—although a significant number in this latter group may find themselves eagerly looking for wonder, truth, community, ethics, and discipline, while being unwilling to subject themselves to the injunctions of one or other religion in doing so. For most ordinary believers in India today, irrespective of their specific faiths, religion lies beyond definitions. And yet, it appears to frame social engagements, cultural expressions, political affiliations, civic involvement, even ethical choices. Without knowing it, and certainly without acknowledging it, India approaches religion in a deeply Durkheimian fashion: as a social fabric that provides a moral compass and a sense of collective identity united under the sign of the sacred—'things set apart and forbidden'—a sacred that would often be a (or many) supernatural being(s), but could just as well be the nation itself.

The nation as a sacred entity has been one of the most significant ideas to emerge in modern India. Its roots lie in the ideological discourses around anti-colonial nationalism that mounted a spirited defence of the colonial and evangelical critique of Indian religion, society, and culture. Its historical emergence owes a debt to the manner in which India's majority religion, Hinduism, grew in the same period into a homogenous, all-encompassing phenomenon taking under its vast and 'eternal' umbrella all kinds of traditions and religious expressions that fell outside the Abrahamic fold. And its sophisticated articulation came from the writings of figures who were looking for a concept of a nation, and a political theology to uphold that nation, outside Western civilizational frameworks. In a series of lectures delivered in 1965 titled *ekatma manavavaad* (integral humanism), Pandit Deendayal Upadhyaya, a leader of the Rashtriya Swayamsevak Sangh (RSS) and one of the most sophisticated thinkers of nation and religion (as dharma), has this to say: 'The laws that help manifest and maintain Chiti [soul] of a nation are termed Dharma of that nation ... If Dharma is destroyed, the nation perishes. Anyone who abandons Dharma, betrays the nation ... Dharma is not confined to temples and mosques ... Dharma is much wider ... We have always vested sovereignty in Dharma' (Upadhyaya 1965: 152–157). What Upadhyaya is arguing for is, in an important manner, a Hindu (or, more specifically, dharmic) articulation of what Charles Schmitt termed as political theology in his 1934 classic on the subject. 'All significant concepts of the modern day theory of the state,' Schmitt noted, 'are secularized theological concepts' (Schmitt 1985: 36). They are 'transferred from theology to the theory of the state', such as where Upadhyaya emphatically notes the upholding of 'soul of the nation' or *chiti* as the basis of *dharmarajya*—a sovereignty that operates within the ambit of dharma.

It is fairly clear that religion in contemporary India cannot be separated from its entanglement with the project of nation-building. Neither can it be parsed out from the strong embeddedness within social identities and community formation. Indeed, it is possible to see political theology and social identities as two sides of the same coin in this regard, where the former provides the ideological basis for the strengthening of the latter. What, if anything, can the gleanings from comparative religion, with its commitment to interfaith relations, dialogue, and understanding every religion in principle as equal offer in this regard?

A comparative approach towards religions must accept as a given that while religion is a central human phenomenon and experience, it is not necessarily or even uniquely tied to a civilizational framework. Religion does not constitute civilizational homogeneity of a nation, just as race, ethnicities, languages, and the choice of clothes that we wear do not. This is despite the large volume of writings linking each one of these to something that is essential, civilizational, and, in the context of India, also eternal. The presence of multiple religious communities within India, each with practices that are divergent from the scripturally sanctioned ones, is testimony to the fact that people's everyday religious lives are often deeply at odds with the larger ideological purposes that religion is often made to play in the life of a nation.

At the same time, and perhaps in part due to the social segregation that we see in India, both inter- and intra-religious interaction and engagement between different regional, linguistic, class- and caste-based articulations are limited. Interfaith dialogue within a respectful setting is a significant aspect of comparative religions, and several scholars of comparative religions have also avidly engaged with multiple religious traditions in their own work and, at times, in their own lives as well. Social and infrastructural challenges notwithstanding, we must collectively agree to engage respectfully with multiple religious traditions, while holding a critical light to our own. For the primary contentions between religions today are not theological (regarding the unity or not of god/s) or soteriological (regarding afterlife), but social (regarding cohabitation) and political (regarding equal rights for all, irrespective of religious, or other, affiliations).

Hence, the challenge for religion in contemporary India can be mapped on to the following three registers: pluralism, emancipation, and tolerance. Each presents us with theoretical as well as practical dimensions. Thus, religious pluralism brings into focus the manner in which the principle of secularism is understood as well as constitutionally worked out and implemented through policy and law. Religious emancipation relates, on the one hand, to social and political emancipation—consisting of equal rights, freedoms, and dignity—and, on the other hand, to the broader questions of other-worldly concerns and salvation that come together in liberation theologies within different religious traditions. And tolerance invites us to think about coexistence as a political project, a civic necessity, and an ethical framework, while understanding each other's religious beliefs and practices through interfaith dialogue.

Let me elaborate on each of these. Religious pluralism, simply speaking, refers to an acknowledgement that there is more than one religion, and that no religion predominates in the state or in public and civic life. Pluralism is the core principle of democracy in several different ways. In the Indian context, religious pluralism lies at the core of the working of its democracy. While in principle the idea of pluralism is both enshrined in the Constitution and reiterated by the conscience-keepers of the nation through invoking phrases such as *sarva dharma samabhava*, its real-world articulations are yet to be fully fleshed out. Modern Indian religious thinkers and actors such as Ramakrishna, Gandhi, and Vinoba Bhave have demonstrated a deep religious pluralism through leading a life that exemplifies the same. However, notions of civilizational and cultural superiority, located in various strains of Indic thought, have often overlooked the importance of deep pluralism for Indian social and civic life.

In many ways, the second challenge, emancipation, often stands in conflict to the easy and superficial practice of pluralism. Emancipation draws attention to the question of social, political, and spiritual freedoms and offers specific religions as inherently more or less appropriate on those grounds. However, a close scrutiny of every religion in India demonstrates that while spiritual emancipation is a core teaching, social and political emancipation as understood through the lens of dignity and equality requires regular attention and work, by both religious leaders as well as every-day practitioners. More recently, the idea of liberation theology has brought to centre stage the idea that religion can and should serve as the source and moral thrust for social and political emancipation as much as it does for spiritual emancipation. It is, in this con-text, important to acknowledge that every religion has its own liberation theology wherein ideas of deep humanism and respect can exist alongside discussions around salvation and release.

Finally, tolerance. While recent scholars have critiqued tolerance as merely a form of 'regulating aversion', it is important to accept that even in this most narrowly defined manner, tolerance is the basic minimum necessity for coexistence in a plural society. However, when placed alongside other values such as neighbourliness, compassion, non-violence—values that are core doctrinal aspects of several of the world's religions—tolerance can turn into a deeper disposi-tion that extends beyond its function of regulating aversion. The importance of interfaith dialogue and communication is absolutely necessary in this regard.

Scholars of religion provide us with numerous examples of such cross-faith dialogue in Indian history. At times, it takes place through translations of core religious concepts and ideas into indigenous terms, for example, the prophet understood through the identifiably Vaishnava Hindu concept of an *avatara* in Tamil and Hindustani literature from the late medieval period. At other times, it emerges from a shared vocabulary of concepts and the worlds of labour that find their way into religious articulations across faiths—the unstruck sound, the hall of mirrors, the palace-like body, the swan-soul, the beloved pining for his/her lover—all of which form tropes and metaphors that fill the world of popular religious songs. That the lived religious worlds may not be that different from each other is recounted in *Hindu-Turk Samvad* ('Dialogue between a Hindu and a Turk'), composed by Eknath, a sixteenth-century Maratha poet-saint. After considerable back and forth on the doctrinal and practised aspects of their respective religions, Eknath ends his dialogue with the words *ekyavakya vivada, vivadi jahala anuvada* ('the debate was about the articulating the One; through debate, they understood each other').

If we are as a nation able to take argument to mutual understanding, and to approach our individual and collective religious lives through the perspective of pluralism, emancipation, and tolerance, it would be possible for us to go beyond the limitations of a narrowly understood secularism and aim for a social and civic life where religion is neither absent nor merely instrumental to other things.

Bibliography and Further Reading

Preface

McCutcheon, Russell T. 1997. *Manufacturing Religion: The Discourse on Sui Generis Religion and the Politics of Nostalgia.* New York: Oxford University Press.

Masuzawa, Tomoko. 2005. *The Invention of World Religions, or, How European Universalism Was Preserved in the Language of Pluralism.* Chicago: University of Chicago Press.

Narayanan, Vasudha. 2015. 'The History of the Academic Study of Religion in Universities, Centers, Institutes in India'. *Numen* 62: 7–39.

Press Information Bureau. 2015. 'RGI Releases Census 2011 Data on Population by Religious Communities'. Government of India, Ministry of Home Affairs. Available at https://pib.gov.in/newsite/printrelease. aspx?relid=126326#:~:text=Total%20Population%20 in%202011%20is,Stated%200.29%20crores%20 (0.2%25), accessed 29 September 2024.

Sharpe, Eric J. 1975. *Comparative Religion (A Story)*. London: Duckworth.

Introduction

Ambedkar, B. R. (2014). *Annihilation of Caste: The Annotated Critical Edition*. New Delhi: Navayana Publishing. (First published in 1936).

Balagangadhara, S. N. 1994. *The Heathen in His Blindness: Asia, the West, and the Dynamic of Religion*. Leiden: E. J. Brill.

Banerjee, Prathama. 2017. 'Ambedkar's Rethinking of Religion'. *Forward Press*. Available at https://www.forwardpress.in/2017/05/ambedkars-rethinking-of-religion/, accessed 27 October 2024.

Chidester, David. 2014. *Empire of Religion: Imperialism and Comparative Religion*. Chicago: University of Chicago Press.

Durkheim, Émile. 1995. *The Elementary Forms of Religious Life*. Trans. Karen E. Fields. New York: The Free Press. First published in French in 1912.

Freud, Sigmund. 1961. *The Future of an Illusion*. Tr. James Strachey. New York: W. W. Norton & Co. First published in German in 1927.

Geetha, V., and Rajadurai, S. V. 1998. *Towards a Non-Brahmin Millennium: From Iyothee Thass to Periyar*. Delhi: Samya.

James, William. 1902. *The Varieties of Religious Experience*. Longmans, Green & Co.

King, Richard. 2013. *Orientalism and Religion: Postcolonial Theory, India, and the 'Mystic East'.* London: Routledge.

Metcalf, Thomas. 1997. *Ideologies of the Raj.* Berkeley and Los Angeles: University of California Press.

Otto, Rudolph. 1923. *The Idea of the Holy. London:* Oxford University Press. First published in German in 1917.

Pals, Daniel L. 2006. *Eight Theories of Religion.* New York: Oxford University Press.

Radhakrishnan, S. 1927. *The Hindu View of Life.* London: George Allen and Unwin.

Rao, K. L. Seshagiri. 1978. *Mahatma Gandhi and Comparative Religion.* Delhi: Motilal Banarsidass.

Sevea, Iqbal Singh. 2012. *The Political Philosophy of Muhammad Iqbal.* New York: Cambridge University Press.

Smith, Wilfred Cantwell. 1962/1991. *The Meaning and End of Religion.* New York: The Macmillan Company.

Tagore, Rabindranath. 1931/2022. *The Religion of Man: International Edition.* New York: Monkfish.

Chapter 1. Religion, Modernity, Identity

Ahmad, Hilal. 2019. *Siyasi Muslims: A Story of Political Islams in India.* Delhi: Penguin.

Anderson, Walter K., and Damle, Shridhar D. 1987. *Brotherhood in Saffron: The Rashtriya Swayamsevak Sangh and Hindu Revivalism.* New Delhi: Vistaar Publications.

Beckerlegge, Gwilym. 2008. *Colonialism, Modernity, Religious Identities: Religious Reform Movements in South Asia*. Oxford: Oxford University Press.

Breckenridge, Carol A., and van der Veer, Peter, eds. 1993. *Orientalism and the Postcolonial Predicament: Perspectives on South Asia*. Philadelphia: University of Pennsylvania Press.

Chandramohan, P. 2016. *Developmental Modernity in Kerala: Narayana Guru, SNDP Yogam and Social Reform*. Delhi: Tulika Books.

Cohn, Bernard S. 1987. *An Anthropologist among the Historians and Other Essays*. Delhi: Oxford University Press.

Dalmia, Vasudha. 1997. *The Nationalization of Hindu Traditions: Bhartendu Harishchandra and Nineteenth-Century Banaras*. Oxford: Oxford University Press.

Dalmia, Vasudha. 2003. *Orienting India: European Knowledge Formation in the Eighteenth and Nineteenth Centuries*. New Delhi: Three Essays Press.

Datta, Pradip Kumar. 1999. *Carving Blocs: Communal Ideology in Early Twentieth-century Bengal*. Delhi: Oxford University Press.

Davis, Richard H. 2015. *The Bhagavad Gita: A Biography*. Princeton: Princeton University Press.

Devadevan, Manu V. 2016. *A Pre-History of Hinduism*. Berlin: DeGruyter.

Eaton, Richard M. 1993. *The Rise of Islam and the Bengal Frontier, 1204–1760*. Berkeley and Los Angeles: University of California Press.

Frykenberg, Robert Eric. 1993/2008/2010. *Christianity in India: From Beginnings to the Present*. Oxford: Oxford University Press.

Gilmartin, David, and Lawrence, Bruce. 2000. *Beyond Turk and Hindu: Rethinking Religious Identities in Islamic South Asia*. Gainesville, FL: University Press of Florida.

Green, Nile. 2020. *Global Islam: A Very Short Introduction*. New York: Oxford University Press.

Halbfass, Wilhelm. 1988. *India and Europe: An Essay in Understanding*. Albany: SUNY Press.

Hatcher, Brian A. 2014. *Bourgeois Hinduism, or, Faith of the Modern Vedantists: Rare Discourses from Early Colonial Bengal*. Oxford: Oxford University Press.

Hatcher, Brian A., ed. 2016. *Hinduism in the Modern World*. New York: Routledge.

Inden, Ronald B. 1990. *Imagining India*. Oxford: Basil Blackwell.

Jaffrelot, Christophe. 1996/1999. *The Hindu Nationalist Movement and Indian Politics: 1925 to the 1990s*. Delhi: Penguin.

Jondhale, Surendra, and Beltz, Johannes, eds. 2004. *Reconstructing the World: B. R. Ambedkar and Buddhism in India*. New Delhi: Oxford University Press.

Jones, Kenneth W. 1975. *Arya Dharm: Hindu Consciousness in 19th-Century Punjab*. Berkeley and Los Angeles: University of California Press.

Jones, Kenneth W. 1989. *Socio-Religious Reform Movements in British India*. Cambridge: Cambridge University Press.

Juergensmeyer, Mark. 1982. *Religion as a Social Vision: The Movement Against Untouchability in 20th-Century Punjab.* Berkeley and Los Angeles: University of California Press.

Kaviraj, Sudipta. 1997. 'Religion and Identity in India'. *Ethnic and Racial Studies* 20(2): 325–44.

Lee, Joel. 2021. *Deceptive Majority: Dalits, Hinduism, and Underground Religion.* Cambridge: Cambridge University Press.

Lelyveld, David. 1975. *Aligarh's First Generation: Muslim Solidarity in British India.* Princeton: Princeton University Press.

Menon, Dilip. 2002. 'Religion and Colonial Modernity: Rethinking Belief and Modernity'. *Economic and Political Weekly* 37(17): 1662–7.

Metcalf, Barbara. 1982. *Islamic Revival in British India: Deoband 1860–1900.* Princeton: Princeton University Press.

Oberoi, Harjot. 1994. *The Construction of Religious Boundaries: Culture, Identity, and Diversity in the Sikh Tradition.* Chicago: University of Chicago Press.

ORGI (Office of the Registrar General and Census Commissioner of India). 2011. 'Distribution of Population by Religions'. Drop-in Articles on Census, No. 4. Available at https://censusindia.gov.in/census. website/data/DROPIN, accessed 29 September 2024.

Pandey, Gyanendra. 1990/2006. *The Construction of Communalism in Colonial North India.* Delhi: Oxford University Press.

Pandiyan, M. S. S. 2007. *Brahmin and Non-Brahmin: Genealogies of the Tamil Political Present*. Ranikhet: Permanent Black.

Ram, Ronki. 2008. 'Ravidass Deras and Social Protest: Making Sense of Dalit Consciousness in Punjab (India)'. *Journal of Asian Studies* 67: 1341–64.

Robinson, Francis. 2008. 'Islamic Reform and Modernities in South Asia'. *Modern Asian Studies* 42(2/3): 259–81.

Roy, Haimanti. 2018. *The Partition of India*. New Delhi: Oxford University Press.

Savarkar, Vinayak Damodar. 1923. *Who Is a Hindu? Essentials of Hindutva*. India: Hindi Sahitya Sadan.

Sharma, Arvind. 2005. *Modern Hindu Thought: An Introduction*. New Delhi: Oxford University Press.

Yelle, Robert. 2013. *The Language of Disenchantment: Protestant Literalism and Colonial Discourse in British India*. New York: Oxford University Press.

Chapter 2. Religion as Practice

Appadurai, Arjun. 1981. *Worship and Conflict Under Colonial Rule: A South Indian Case*. Cambridge: Cambridge University Press.

Babb, Lawrence. 1975. *Divine Hierarchy: Popular Hinduism in Central India*. New York: Columbia University Press.

Bellamy, Carla. 2011. *The Powerful Ephemeral: Everyday Healing in an Ambiguously Islamic Place*. Berkeley and Los Angeles: University of California Press.

Bhattacharjee, Malini. 2019. *Disaster Relief and the RSS: Resurrecting Religion through Humanitarianism*. Delhi: Sage Publications.

Bloomer, Kirsten. 2018. *Possessed by the Virgin: Hinduism, Roman Catholicism, and Marian Possession in Southern India*. New York: Oxford University Press.

Dempsey, Corinne G. 2001. *Kerala Christian Sainthood: Collisions of Culture and Worldview*. Oxford: Oxford University Press.

Eliade, Mircea. 1959/1987. *The Sacred and the Profane: The Nature of Religion*. Trans. Willard R. Trask. New York: Harcourt. First published in French, 1957.

Feldhaus, Anne. 2003. *Connected Places: Region, Pilgrimage, and Geographical Imagination in India*. New York: Palgrave Macmillan.

Flueckiger, Joyce Burkhalter. 2006. *In Amma's Healing Room: Gender and Vernacular Islam in South India*. Bloomington: Indiana University Press.

Fuller, Christopher J. 1992. *The Camphor Flame: Popular Hinduism and Society in India*. Princeton: Princeton University Press.

Geertz, Clifford. 1966. 'Religion as a Cultural System'. In Michael Parker Banton, ed., *Anthropological Approaches to the Study of Religion*. London: Tavistock, 1–46.

Ibrahim, Farhana, ed. 2024. *Studies in Religion and the Everyday*. Oxford: Oxford University Press.

Ilaiah, Kancha. 1996. *Why I Am Not a Hindu: A Shudra Critique of Hindutva Philosophy, Culture, and Political Economy*. Kolkata: Samya.

Iyer, Shriya. 2018. *The Economics of Religion in India.* Cambridge, MA: The Belknap Press of Harvard University Press.

Jeffrey, Robin. 1976. 'Temple-Entry Movement in Travancore, 1860–1940'. *Social Scientist* 4(8): 3–27.

Mohammad, Afsar. 2013. *The Festival of Pirs: Popular Islam and Shared Devotion in South India.* New York: Oxford University Press.

Narayan, Kirin. 2011. *Storytellers, Saints, and Scoundrels: Folk Narrative in Hindu Religious Teaching.* Philadelphia: University of Pennsylvania Press.

Pandey, Bhupendra, and Mishra, Dheeraj. 2024. 'Baba's Business: The Godman and His Empire', *Indian Express.* Available at https://indianexpress.com/article/long-reads/hathras-stampede-bhole-baba-narayan-sakaar-hari-kasganj-godman-9435984/, accessed 19 August 2024.

Singh, Vikash. 2017. *Uprising of the Fools: Pilgrimage as Moral Protest in Contemporary India.* Stanford, CA: Stanford University Press.

Srinivas, Smriti. 2001. *Landscapes of Urban Memory: The Sacred and the Civic in India's High-Tech City.* Minneapolis: University of Minnesota Press.

Taneja, Anand Vivek. 2018. *Jinnealogies: Time, Islam, and Ecological Thought in the Medieval Ruins of Delhi.* Stanford, CA: Stanford University Press.

Turner, Victor. 1969/2017. *The Ritual Process: Structure and Anti-Structure.* New York: Routledge.

Wadley, Susan S. 2005. *Essays on North Indian Folk Traditions.* New Delhi: Chronicle Books.

Chapter 3. Caste, Sect, and Religion

Ahmad, Imtiaz, ed. 1973/1978. *Caste and Social Stratification amongst Muslims in India.* Delhi: Manohar.

Aktor, Mikael. 2018. 'Social Classes: *Varna*'. In Patrick Olivelle and Donald R. Davies, Jr., eds., *Hindu Law: A New History of the* Dharmasastras. Oxford: Oxford University Press, 60–77.

Ambedkar, B. R. 1936/2014. *The Annihilation of Caste: The Annotated Critical Edition*, ed. S. Anand. Delhi: Verso Books.

Ambedkar, B. R. 2011. *The Buddha and His Dhamma: A Critical Edition*, ed. Aakash Singh Rathore and Ajay Verma. New Delhi: Oxford University Press.

Ansari, Khalid Anis. 2023. 'Revisiting the Minority Imagination: An Inquiry into the Anticaste Pasmanda-Muslim Discourse in India'. *Critical Philosophy of Race* 11(1): 120–47.

Azam, Shireen. 2023. 'Scheduled Caste Status for Dalit Muslims and Christians: A Comprehensive Clarification'. *Economic and Political Weekly* 58(27): 14–19.

Babb, Lawrence. 2006. 'Sects in Indian Religions'. In Veeda Das, ed., *Handbook of Indian Sociology.* New Delhi: Oxford University Press, 223–40.

Bandyopadhyay, Sekhar. 2004. *Caste, Culture, and Hegemony: Social Domination in Colonial Bengal.* New Delhi: Sage.

Dirks, Nicholas. 2001. *Castes of Mind: Colonialism and the Making of Modern India.* Princeton: Princeton University Press.

Dumont, Louis. 1970/1999. *Homo Hierarchicus: The Caste System and Its Implications.* Trans. Mark Sainsbury, Louis Dumont, and Basia Gulati. New Delhi: Oxford University Press. First published in French in 1966.

Gold, Daniel. 1982. *The Lord as Guru in North Indian Religion: Hindi Sant Tradition and Universals of Religious Perception.* Chicago: University of Chicago Press.

Guha, Sumit. 2013. *Beyond Caste: Identity and Power in South Asia, Past and Present.* Leiden: Brill.

Gupta, Dipankar, ed. 2004. *Caste in Question: Identity or Hierarchy?* New Delhi: Sage Publications.

Jodhka, Surinder S. 2012. *Caste.* New Delhi: Oxford University Press.

Keune, Jon. 2021. *Shared Devotion, Shared Food: Equality and the Bhakti-Caste Question in North India.* New York: Oxford University Press.

Lorenzen, David N. 1987. 'Traditions of Non-Caste Hinduism: The Kabir Panth'. *Contributions to Indian Sociology* 21(2): 263–83.

Madan, Triloki N. 1987. *Non-Renunciation: Themes and Interpretations of Hindu Culture.* Delhi: Oxford University Press.

Narayan, Badri. 2009. *Fascinating Hindutva: Saffron Politics and Dalit Mobilisation*. New Delhi: Sage Publications.

Omvedt, Gail. 2003. *Buddhism in India: Challenging Brahmanism and Caste*. New Delhi: Sage.

Omvedt, Gail. 2008. *Seeking Begumpura: The Social Vision of Anti-Caste Intellectuals*. New Delhi: Navayana.

Ram, Ronki. 2007. 'Social Exclusion, Resistance, and the Deras: Exploring the Myth of Casteless Sikh Society in Punjab'. *Economic and Social Weekly* 42 (40): 4066–74.

Singh, Nikki Gurinder Kaur. 2011. *Sikhism: An Introduction*. London: I. B. Tauris.

Srinivas, M. N. 1962. *Caste in Modern India and Other Essays*. Bombay: Asia Publishing House.

Vajpeyi, Ananya. 2010. '*Sudradharma* and Legal Treatments of Caste'. In Timothy Lubin, Donald R. Davis, and Jayanth Krishnan, eds., *Hinduism and Law: An Introduction*. Cambridge: Cambridge University Press, 154–66.

Viswanath, Rupa. 2014. *The Pariah Problem: Caste, Religion, and the Social in Modern India*. New York: Columbia University Press.

Chapter 4. Law and Religion

Ahsan, Sofi. 2024. 'Muslims Cannot Claim Right to Live-In Relationships: Against Their Customary Law—Allahabad High Court'. *Bar and Bench*.

Available at https://www.barandbench.com/news/ muslims-cannot-claim-right-live-in-relationship-agai nst-customary-law-allahabad-high-court, accessed 29 September 2024.

Bagchi, S. C. 1933. *Juristic Personality of Hindu Deities.* Calcutta: University of Calcutta.

Baird, Robert, D., ed. 1995/2005. *Religion and Law in Independent India.* New Delhi: Manohar.

Bhargava, Rajeev. 2002. 'What Is Indian Secularism and What Is It For?'. *India Review* 1(1): 1–32.

Bhatia, Gautam. 2022. 'Uniform Civil Code: Reframe the Debate.' *Hindustan Times.* Available at https://www. hindustantimes.com/opinion/uniform-civil-code-refr ame-the-debate-101672152817099.html. Accessed 28 March 2025.

Chandhoke, Neera. 2019. *Rethinking Pluralism, Secularism, and Tolerance: Anxieties of Coexistence.* New Delhi: Sage.

Chatterjee, Nandini. 2011. *The Making of Indian Secularism: Empire, Law, and Christianity, 1830–1960.* New York: Palgrave Macmillan.

Chatterjee, Nandini. 2020. *Negotiating Mughal Law: A Family of Landlords across Three Indian Empires.* Cambridge: Cambridge University Press.

Derrett, J. Duncan M. 1963. *Introduction to Modern Hindu Law.* London: Oxford University Press.

Fuller, Christopher J. 1988. 'Hinduism and Scriptural Authority in Modern Indian Law'. *Comparative Studies in Society and History* 30(2): 225–48.

John, Mathew. 2023. *India's Communal Constitution: Law, Religion, and the Making of a People.* Cambridge: Cambridge University Press.

Kapur, Ratna. 2023. 'The Ayodhya Case, Freedom of Religion, and the Making of Modernist "Hinduism"'. *Contemporary South Asia.* DOI: 10.1080/09584935.2023.2227127.

Lhost, Elizabeth. 2022. *Everyday Islamic Law and the Making of Modern South Asia.* Chapel Hill: University of North Carolina Press.

Lubin, Timothy, Davis, Donald J., and Krishnan, Jayanth K. 2010. *Hinduism and Law: An Introduction.* Cambridge: Cambridge University Press.

Nair, Janaki. 1996. *Women and Law in Colonial India.* New Delhi: Kali for Women.

Nandy, Asish. 1995. 'An Anti-Secularist Manifesto'. *Economic and Political Weekly* 22(1): 35–64.

Olivelle, Patrick, and Davis, Donald J. Jr., eds. 2018. *Hindu Law: A New History of Dharmaśāstra.* Oxford: Oxford University Press.

Sen, Ronojoy. 2010/2019. *Articles of Faith: Religion, Secularism and the Indian Supreme Court.* New Delhi: Oxford University Press.

Sethi, Manisha. 2019. 'Communities and Courts: Religion and Law in Modern India'. *South Asian History and Culture* 10(2): 109–23.

Tejani, Shabnum. 2007. *Indian Secularism: A Social and Intellectual History 1890–1950*. Ranikhet: Permanent Black.

Chapter 5. Media and Religious Publics

Bhatia, Varuni. 2020. 'Shani on the Web: Virality and Vitality in Digital Popular Hinduism'. *Religion* 11(1): 456. doi:10.3390/rel11090456.

Bhrugubanda, Uma Maheshwari. 2018. *Deities and Devotees: Cinema, Religion and Politics in South India*. New Delhi: Oxford University Press.

Davis, Richard H. 1997/2012. *Lives of Indian Images*. Princeton: Princeton University Press.

Dwyer, Rachel. 2006. *Filming the Gods: Religion and Indian Cinema*. New York: Routledge.

Jain, Kajri. 2007. *Gods in the Bazaar: The Economies of Indian Calendar Art*. Durham, NC: Duke University Press.

Jeffrey, Robin. 2021. 'Media in Religion and Politics'. *Economic and Political Weekly Engage* 56(3): 2–11. Available at https://www.epw.in/engage/article/media-relig ion-and-politics, accessed 10 February 2025.

Jeffrey, Robin, and Doron, Assa. 2013. *Cell Phone Nation: How Mobile Phones Have Revolutionized Business, Politics, and Everyday Lives in India*. Gurgaon: Hachette India.

Lutgendorf, Philip. 1990. 'Ramayan: The Video'. *Drama Review* 34(2): 127–76.

Manuel, Peter M. 1993. *Cassette Culture: Popular Music and Technology in North India*. Chicago: University of Chicago Press.

Metcalf, Barbara D., trans. 1992. *Perfecting Women: Maulana Ashraf 'Ali Thanawi's Bihishti Zewar*. Berkeley and Los Angeles: University of California Press.

Mukul, Akshaya. 2015. *Gita Press and the Making of Hindu India*. Delhi: Harper Collins.

Pinney, Christopher. 2004. *Photos of the Gods: The Printed Image and Political Struggle in India*. London: Reaktion Books.

Prasad, Madhava M. 2009. 'Fan Bhakti and Subaltern Sovereignty: Enthusiasm as a Political Factor'. *Economic and Political Weekly* 64(29): 68–76.

Purohit, Kunal. 2023. *H-Pop: The Secretive World of Hindutva Pop Stars*. Delhi: Harper Collins.

Rajagopal, Arvind. 2001. *Politics After Television: Hindu Nationalism and the Reshaping of the Public in India*. Cambridge: Cambridge University Press.

Raman, P. 2020. 'How the Sangh Parivar Organized the 1995 Ganesh Milk Miracle and Why the Plan Flopped'. *The Wire*. Available at https://thewire.in/religion/ganesh-milk-miracle-1995-sangh-parivar, accessed 15 August 2024.

Ramaswamy, Sumathi, 2010. *The Goddess and the Nation: Mapping Mother India*. Durham, NC: Duke University Press.

Srinivas, S. V. 2013. *Politics as Performance: Social History of Telugu Cinema*. Ranikhet: Permanent Black.

Srinivas, Tulasi. 2018. *Cow in the Elevator: An Anthropology of Wonder*. Durham, NC: Duke University Press.

Stolow, Jeremy, ed. 2013. *Deus in Machina: Religion, Technology, and the Things in Between*. New York: Fordham University Press.

Thomas, Pradip Ninan. 2008. *Strong Religion, Zealous Media: Christian Fundamentalism and Communication in India*. New Delhi: Sage.

Udupa, Sahana. 2018. 'Enterprise Hindutva and Social Media in Urban India'. *Contemporary South Asia* 26 (4): 453–67.

Zeiler, Xenia, ed. 2020. *Digital Hinduism*. New York: Routledge.

Religion and the Nation

Jaffrelot, Christophe, ed., 2007. *Hindu Nationalism: A Reader*. Princeton: Princeton University Press.

Schmitt, Carl. 1934/1985. *Political Theology: Four Chapters on the Concept of Sovereignty*. Trans. George Schwab. Cambridge, MA: MIT Press.

Index

For the benefit of digital users, indexed terms that span two pages (e.g., 52–53) may, on occasion, appear on only one of those pages.

About the Author

Varuni Bhatia is a historian of religion, specializing in modern Hinduism and bhakti traditions. She is currently Professor of History at the School of Arts and Sciences, Azim Premji University, Bengaluru. Her first book, *Unforgetting Chaitanya: Vaishnavism and Cultures of Devotion in Colonial Bengal* (Oxford University Press, 2017), explored how Bengali Vaishnava traditions were transformed and integrated into middle-class, cultural nationalist frameworks. Bhatia's ongoing research looks at the emergence of Hindu esotericism as an integral aspect of Hindu modernity, with a focus on Hindu nationalism and anti-colonial movements. She has also published articles on digital Hinduism, especially how popular beliefs and practices continue to proliferate over social media platforms and influence everyday religious practices.

01 14

The manufacturer's authorised representative in the EU for product
safety is Oxford University Press España S.A. of El Parque Empresarial
San Fernando de Henares, Avenida de Castilla, 2 - 28830 Madrid
(www.oup.es/en or product.safety@oup.com). OUP España S.A. also acts
as importer into Spain of products made by the manufacturer.
Printed and bound by CPI Group (UK) Ltd, Croydon, CR0 4YY

16/12/2025

02020469-0001